# Country Furniture

## *and Accessories from Quebec*

Warren I. Johansson

1469 Morstein Road, West Chester, Pennsylvania 19380

To Dot
and
Fred, Peter, and Sally
Happy Memories

Published by Schiffer Publishing, Ltd.
1469 Morstein Road
West Chester, Pennsylvania 19380
Please write for a free catalog.
This book may be purchased from the publisher.
Please include $2.00 postage.
Try your bookstore first.

Printed in the United States of America.
ISBN: 0-88740-276-3

# Contents

Contents

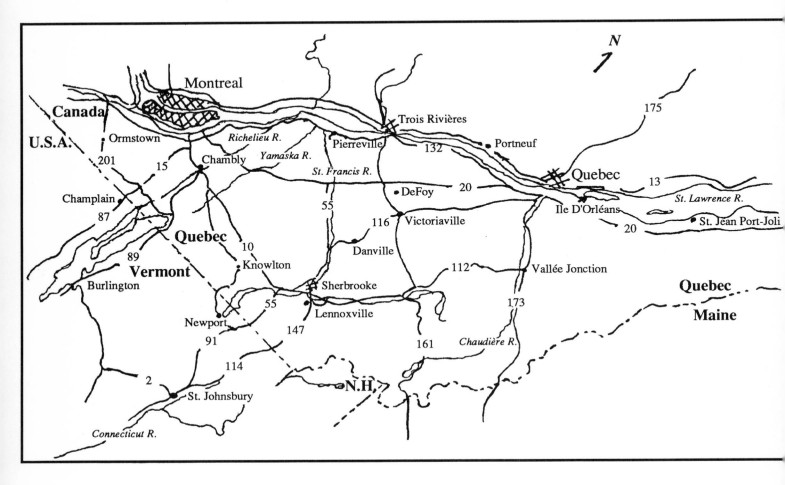

A regional map showing key highways, waterways, and many locations mentioned in this book. Much of the region east of the Yamaska River Valley, west of the Chaudière River, and south of the Transcanadian highway (auto Route 20) to the international border constitutes the Eastern Townships.

# Acknowledgments

If it were not for the generosity of many collectors, dealers, librarians, archivists, and the staff of several museums, who placed their knowledge and extensive resources at our disposal, this book would not have become a reality.

Through the courtesy of many Canadian dealers, we were able to examine and study in detail their extensive stock, and, in several cases, select examples to photograph. We particularly wish to thank René Beaudoin and family of DeFoy, Quebec, Clay Benson, Brian and Joan Damoulin; also Jean Deshaies and Denis Landry of Centre Antiques of Victoriaville, Maurice LeMay, Rodney Lloyd, Georges Poirier, René St. Jean, and all others who shared time and knowledge.

There are several to be remembered and thanked posthumously, including Doris Gale, Colin MacLeod, Frank Riff, and particularly those two hospitable grand ladies, Elsie and Gwen Elliott, for their knowledge and camaraderie around the table over tea.

Thanks also to the Williamsburg Brass Co., Inc., at the Brassworks; Bruce Thomas of DeCoy World; Mountain Crest Antiques, Hadley, Massachusetts; and Monique Shay of Hidden River Farm, Woodbury, Connecticut, for allowing us to examine and photograph some of her large, select stock of French-Canadian antique furniture. The list of dealers in Brimfield, Massachusetts, with Canadian antiques is too long to include here, but we thank all of you for time and knowledge shared.

We wish to extend our deep appreciation to members of the staff of the following museums and libraries who assisted us: Athol Historical Society, Athol, Massachusetts; Ms. Anne Grant of Bishop's University and Champlain Regional Community College, Lennoxville, Quebec; Brome County Historical Museum Archives Center, Knowlton, Quebec; Greenfield Community College Library, Pioneer Valley Studies Center, Greenfield, Massachusetts; Historic Deerfield, Inc., Deerfield, Massachusetts; Lennoxville-Ascot Historical Society Museum, Lennoxville, Quebec.

Also, Le Village Québécois D'Anton, Drummondville, Quebec; Memorial Libraries at Deerfield, Massachusetts; Musée de la Societé D'Historie des Cantons de L'Est, Sherbrooke, Quebec; Musée des Ursulines, Quebec; Musée du Quebec, Quebec; Musée de la Civilisation du Québec and its Conservatrice, Ms. Therese LaTour for permission to use certain color prints of furniture from the Musée collection; and the Château de Ramezay, Montreal. Special thanks is due Philip Zea, curator of Historic Deerfield, Inc., for making available their French-Canadian collection for study and photography, and to David Proper, librarian of the Memorial Libraries at Deerfield for able assistance with library materials, and also to Ms. Jennifer Mange, Curatorial Department Assistant at Historic Deerfield, for her services as a photographer and for providing background data on the Historic Deerfield material selected for use in this book.

In particular, I wish to thank our son, Dr. Peter Johansson, University of Wisconsin-River Falls, for reading and critiquing the manuscript. I am also grateful to Gretchen Watson of the English Department at Greenfield Community College for editorial aid, and most importantly to Ms. Mae Tennyson for set-up, typescription, and editorial comment.

It is with sincere appreciation that we thank Frank Leighton for his skillful photography and generous gift of time.

The collections of Dr. and Mrs. Mark Bergland, Mr. and Mrs. Fred Johansson, Dr. and Mrs. Peter Johansson, Mr. and Mrs. Fred Hellen, Ms. Cynthia Ballantyne, Monique Shay, the Athol (MA) Historical Society, Historic Deerfield, Inc., Musée de la Civilisation du Québec, an anonymous friend and the author provided items for photography. Ms. Patty Fitzmaurice provided the graphics for Plate 2. Plate 1 by the Author.

Our son, Frederick Johansson, shared his expertise by providing technical information on matters of construction and form, as well as a number of photographs and the painting, "End of the Line".

Lewis N. Chase, Sr., contributed to the major restoration of several pieces figured in the text, and Lawrence DeMinico seated a number of the chairs.

And finally, I thank my wife and helpmate, Dorothy, with love and deepest appreciation for her unfailing interest, encouragement, constant companionship, and ability to steer me in the right direction, not an easy task.

# Introduction

Have you ever wondered where the nineteenth-century country furniture found in today's American antique marketplace came from? You might be surprised to learn that all of it did not come from "down Maine," or from "Pennsylvania Dutch country," or even from anywhere in the United States. While some of it may come from the popular containerized lots currently being shipped here from Europe, a significant source of country furniture and accessories marketed in the United States is our neighbor to the north, Quebec. This book was written to serve as a guide to that material culture and about the sources and kinds of Quebec country antiques currently in the United States. It also covers a brief history of the Quebec-American antique trade, as well as personal collecting experiences of the author and his family from the mid 1950s to the early 1980s. In addition, attention is paid to the interesting multi-cultural nature of the settlement pattern that developed in the Eastern Townships of Quebec during the nineteenth century and its effect on the material culture there.

In his tome, *The Early Furniture of French-Canada*, Jean Palardy has documented magnificently the *crème de la crème* of French-Canadian furniture from the seventeenth to the nineteenth centuries. Several articles appearing in *The Magazine Antiques* over a long period of years also have documented some of the best furniture of French-Canada. The illustrations in Palardy's book, *The Magazine Antiques*, and in several other important books are from significant private and museum collections in Canada. Until now, however, a void has existed in that the less sophisticated, mundane, nineteenth century country furniture and accessories of Quebec was left largely unrecorded through photos and text. Quantities of this kind of material were shipped to the United States. This volume should help close the gap by utilizing more than two hundred photographs and illustrations of fresh material in our attempt to document some of the rural and *habitant* furniture of nineteenth century Quebec.

I have focused on some of the handcrafted items (material culture) made by individuals or by small woodworking shops for use in farm- and church-related structures across much of the southern part of the Province. These items were either one-of-a-kind or similar pieces with the usual variations. The abundant and similar mass-produced furniture of the mid- and late-nineteenth century has been left out intentionally. This would include pine, black walnut, and ash cottage furniture found in rural and urban areas on both sides of the international border.

One chapter in particular details many identifying characteristics of Quebec country furniture and accessories. Comparisons with American-made pieces appear frequently throughout the text. This information should prove helpful, since so much material culture has left Quebec and the Canadian identity and provenance has been lost. It was during the 1950s and 1960s, in particular, that quantities of Quebec's nineteenth century country antique pieces were gathered by local pickers and dealers and sold to other Canadian and American dealers and collectors. Many pieces were subsequently dispersed hundreds and thousands of miles away. Untold loads were hauled to Ontario, New England, New York, and Pennsylvania, which in turn meant that some pieces eventually ended up in Oklahoma, Texas, California, or other areas. In many ways, it is similar to the container lots of nineteenth century British and Continental pine antique furniture now arriving and being sold in the United States. If the Quebec pickers and dealers had kept records of where they bought items, and that record passed on to the buyer, we would have a better idea of what township or county was the source. However, this was not done and less than complete was the nature of this particular antique trade during the early years.

Identifying the maker of a piece of Quebec country

furniture is next to impossible, as signatures and initials rarely exist. It is possible, however, to speculate with some degree of certainty on the ethnic identity of a maker, whether French descent, British descent, or American descent. In many cases, this can be determined by the joinery and/or style that was adopted. For example, the post-and-frame construction practiced by the French-Canadians since the seventeenth century and continuing well into the nineteenth century gives strong evidence as to origin, as does the bench bed (*banc lit*) introduced to Quebec by the Irish during the nineteenth century. Also, a bicultural approach can be seen in some pieces of furniture in which the inspiration is drawn from more than one culture. The example that comes to mind is the incorporation into one chair of an American-style rabbit-ear Windsor chair back and a French-Canadian *habitant* chair base. Style and joinery can point to the provenance of some furniture too. Rabbit-ear Windsor chairs and simple, four-spindle, plank-seat chairs, as well as ladder-back chairs made of round stock, Windsor-style church benches, and dovetailed or butted-and-nailed blanket boxes with boot-jack ends found in southernmost Quebec most likely were inspired by American examples. Some may have come across the border. Jointed chairs (of mortise-and-tenon construction) are restricted to the vicinity of Quebec City, Côte de Beaupré and the Ile d'Orleans. On the other hand, there are many other Quebec pieces seen in shops and collections whose exact provenance remains elusive. No doubt some pieces have in-migrated from eastern Ontario and New Brunswick, where there are large French-Canadian populations. Other pieces are virtually identical to pieces made outside of Canada, even across the Atlantic.

The inspiration for this book is due in part to experiences that began in 1956. It was in the summer of that year when my family and I began collecting Quebec country antiques. Then as now, we were fascinated by the activities of pickers, dealers, and collectors. Over the years, we have sought answers to many questions regarding the history of nineteenth century antiques. Our interest and knowledge of Quebec culture has grown in the course of thirty years, and we would like to share our findings with collectors of North American antiques. During those years, we talked to scores of dealers, collectors, and museum and library personnel, visited many museums, and traveled thousands of miles gathering information. I have written for all people who share a common interest, enthusiasm, and camaraderie in their love of country antiques. Some American owners of antiques may be surprised to find that their furniture is not "Pennsylvania Dutch," but of Canadian ancestry. It is hoped that other Americans and those of French-Canadian descent may become more aware of the richness of their cultural heritage. The antique collector and student of antiques will find that not only is the material culture of Quebec derived from a long-established French population in the St. Lawrence, Chaudière, and Richelieu Valleys, but also from Irish, Scottish, English, and American traditions, established in the late-eighteenth and first half of the nineteenth centuries. This has resulted in a more varied and richer material culture than first suspected.

**Photography Credits**

Historic Deerfield, Jennifer Mange, photographer: 12, 13, 63, 133, 147, 208; Helga Studio Photographer: 153

Frederick E. Johansson: 10, 53, 67, 167, 187, 188, 211

Frank E. Leighton: 1, 4, 5, 6, 7, 8, 9, 14, 15, 16, 18, 19, 20, 21, 22, 23, 24, 25, 26, 27, 28, 30, 31, 32, 41, 49, 50, 54, 55, 61, 64, 65, 68, 73, 74, 75, 76, 77, 78, 79, 80, 82, 83, 84, 85, 89, 90, 91, 94, 95, 98, 99, 100, 101, 102, 103, 104, 105, 106, 107, 108, 109, 110, 112, 113, 114, 115, 117, 118, 119, 121, 123, 124, 126, 131, 135, 136, 138, 139, 140, 142, 143, 149, 152, 154, 155, 157, 158, 159, 160, 161, 162, 163, 164, 165, 166, 169, 170, 173, 174, 175, 176, 177, 178, 179, 180, 181, 182, 183, 184, 185, 186, 189, 190, 191, 192, 193, 194, 195, 196, 197, 198, 199, 201, 202, 206, 207, 209, 210, 212, 213, 214

All others by the author.

CHAPTER ONE

# The Quebec Antique Connection

I first became aware of the large shipments of antiques coming into New England from Quebec when I was working as a geologist in northern Vermont and New Hampshire from 1956-1960. Canadian antiques were piled on porches of pickers and expediters and in sheds and barns of the New Hampshire towns of Lancaster, Lisbon, and West Lebanon, and in the Norwich, Vermont, area. As it turned out, others were arriving regularly at various dealers' shops in the Connecticut Valley area of Massachusetts, particularly in Greenfield and Northampton. In fact, trucks loaded with flax wheels from the north were commonplace. Three kinds of items seemed to predominate: large-wheel flax wheels, a variety of cupboards, and stretcher-base tables. The cupboards and tables were quite large; some might be described as cumbersome. However, their sturdy construction and high aesthetic potential attracted my attention.

Together with my family, we spent some of our spare time seeking the more exact sources of these exciting, sometimes rough, specimens. We visited a colleague in Island Pond, Vermont, whose friend had found a place in Danville, Quebec, where flax wheels could be purchased in 1957 for $5.00 each. This tip led us into Quebec and Quebec City. We had a lot to learn.

First, there were no traditional roadside antique shops such as we were used to in New England, New York, and Pennsylvania. Secondly, because we initially could not identify the old houses and barns, we had to learn about what they and their dependencies looked like in Quebec. It was difficult to locate dealers and/or pickers in the country. At that time, there existed but a few long-established dealers in the major cities, such as S. Breitman's in Montreal. We drove from Coaticook to Quebec City via Black Lake and never saw an antique shop. It was hard to know where to begin. We returned from Quebec City driving along the south side of the St.

Lawrence for a long distance westerly before turning south to Victoriaville. We were heartened to see old stone farmhouses near the St. Lawrence but never saw an identifiable antique shop.

Our friend had mentioned the place in Danville, so we stopped there on our way from Victoriaville to Sherbrooke. Danville turned out to be our gateway to success. There were English-speaking people at a store in the center of town, and in a matter of minutes, we received explicit directions from them on how to find the Elliott sisters, who sold antiques at an old farm near Nicolet Falls. When we saw the sign "Antiques" pointing down a maple-shaded lane, we instinctively turned in.

To our right, not more than two hundred feet down the lane, the whole picture began to crystallize. There were at least fifty dough boxes and an equal number of massive cradles in all stages of condition sitting on the slope close to the first of several buildings. To the left, not more than 200 feet away, was the 1830s homestead of the Elliott sisters. Nearby, and parked in a jumbled fashion, were several cars and trucks, with people busily loading and unloading. To the southwest, there were two large barns, and to the south of the house, a shed, a barn, and chicken coops. All of these buildings were packed with antiques in-the-rough. The acre-size field to the southeast of the large barns was also filled, mostly with cupboards and/or *armoires* of all kinds. I shall never forget the enormous size of some of them. The loft of the first of the two large barns was filled with *habitant* chairs of every description.

To the north of this barn was a shed with a little porch, and on that porch sat Gwen Elliott. Inside were her prize collections of glass, china, and metalware. Miss Gwen remained our friend for the next 19 years, until her death in 1976. Her sister Elsie was busy in the house totaling a bill for an Ontario dealer. Our friendship with Elsie continued until her death in 1982.

As it turned out, the tip given to us by a friend in Island Pond led us to the heart of the country antique business in Quebec. It centered around the Elliott sisters. Their interest had been fostered by their father many years before when he began to amass a fine collection of cranberry glass, notably lamps and vessels. After World War II, the Elliott sisters began in earnest. In the early 1950s, they, with the help of numerous pickers (many of whom they educated), brought antiques from farms and villages to Danville from much of the Province. The French-Canadian pickers knew their way around the farms and countryside and were able to buy for virtually nothing discarded pieces that languished in sheds, barns, and other farm dependencies. Most of the pickers arrived on Fridays, and the Elliotts advised us to be at their place then for the best selection. On several occasions, we were there on a Friday and watched the serious, although amusing, haggling that took place between the Elliotts and the pickers. And the Elliotts bought most of what was brought to them, because, after all, they wanted the pickers to return.

While our interest has always centered around well-fashioned country furniture, it seems appropriate at this time to mention some of the other items that the Elliotts had accumulated. They had in stock at any given time an extensive amount (perhaps 500 pieces) of carnival glass, hundreds of pressed glass kerosene lamps, several dozen hanging, brass-framed lamps, scores of sugar molds and butter pats, at least 100 sets of washbowls and pitchers (plate 20), and quantities of the ubiquitous flax wheel. Their porch on the north side of the house became a repository for water benches, duck decoys, and unusual pieces in the later years of their business. The cellar bulged with many small items too. (It should be mentioned that some very fine and relatively expensive *armoires*, including diamond-point cupboards, were being grabbed up by Canadian dealers and collectors during the late 1950s and early 1960s.)

Every week during the warm weather, shipments left for the States and western Ontario by truck, and I have been told that it was not unusual in the 1950s for railroad boxcars loaded with spinning and flax wheels to be shipped to Pennsylvania and to the nearby Washington, DC, area.

During the summer of 1963, I visited a number of country antique shops in eastern Pennsylvania and found Quebec antiques being passed off as Pennsylvania rural pieces, some called Pennsylvania "Dutch." It is true that some Canadian pieces do strongly resemble Pennsylvania rural furniture and could pass very well as such. I recall a dispute with a dealer who insisted that his material was from nearby farms. He was at a loss to explain how a sheet of a French language, Montreal newspaper could be pasted to the underside of some shelves in one of his cupboards. To me, it was obvious that we were looking at a Canadian piece whose shelves had been turned over and the newspaper lining never had been removed. I have found so many old pieces with sheets of newsprint or pages from books or magazines used as lining that it is almost a rule of thumb that a printed paper of some sort will be found in uncleaned cupboards. Thus, in addition to the constructional features which will be described later, the paper remnants can serve today as a good key to the piece's geographical origin.

There were other early country dealers in Quebec; i.e., those who were established at least 35 years or more ago. Surely, two pioneers would be Georges Poirier in Victoriaville and Maurice LeMay in Sherbrooke. In our estimation, however, the big-volume dealers in country antiques for the 1950s were the Elliott sisters. They were the "Quebec antique connection."

In the early 1960s, the pattern changed. A new interest on the part of the Quebec citizenry in antiques, folklore, and Canadian culture resulted from the growing national affluence and extensive government-sponsored cultural programs. Many of the pickers now opened their own shops with a particular concentration developing in the Defoy area, not far from the Trans-Canada Highway (autoroute 20). The Beaudoin family was among the first in that area to develop a large-scale wholesale/retail operation. Today there are several major suppliers of country antiques along the Trans-Canada Highway between Drummondville and Laurier Station. In more recent years, some dealers have tapped their extensive warehouses for furniture parts and architectural fragments to be used with other pieces to rebuild complete specimens. Others are also manufacturing fine reproductions of French-Canadian antique furniture.

In 1966, twenty-two dealers were listed in the guide map "Antique Dealers in the Province of Quebec" as living in the more rural areas. There were several others who were not listed, including the Elliotts. Today country dealers can be found across the entire southern part of the province. As a consequence of the interest in antiques and the increase in dealership, the supply of good country Quebec antiques has greatly diminished and the prices have continued to rise. Many dealers started importing country antiques from New Brunswick and Nova Scotia in the 1970s, and one with whom I spoke in 1983 was selling early twentieth-century oak imported from southeastern Massachusetts. Ironically, some Canadian dealers are now buying regularly in New England the very antiques which were sold out of Quebec years before.

Nonetheless, antiques from Quebec continue to arrive in New England, New York, and many other states, as well as Ontario and other Canadian provinces (although much less frequently than before) via such New England inland routes as routes I-91, I-89, and Rt. 27 and U.S. 201 in Maine, the Trans-Canada Highway, and so on. Generally, high-quality period furniture has come to the States from the Quebec City and Montreal areas since the 1920s and 1930s and country furniture and folk art in quantity since the 1950s.

# CHAPTER TWO

# Lineage, Settlement, and Furniture Styles

Nineteenth-century Quebec country furniture came from a mixed lineage. French-Canada had been undergoing settlement for nearly 200 years by the beginning of the nineteenth century. Until the fall of New France to Great Britain in 1759, Canada was a French colonial country, largely following the social, religious, economic, and cultural dictates of Mother France. Its principle influences had come from France and, to a much lesser degree, the British colonies to the south. However, the geographical isolation of French-Canada, along with its harsh winter climate, had placed from the beginning of settlement an emphasis on the pragmatic way of life, and the embellishments known in France were often dispensed with in Canada. This was true of furniture styles as well as social customs.

By the beginning of the nineteenth century, tastes were changing. The British influence on furniture styles appears well-established, particularly in the larger cities, where mahogany, walnut, and rosewood were preferred. However, the older French styles and techniques of joinery, although modified, continued to be made in the nineteenth century. These older styles persisted for a long time, particularly in more rural French districts. The overall form of *habitant* chairs of many types, for example, changed very little throughout the nineteenth century, and the generous proportions of many *armoires*, low buffets, two-tiered buffets, and commodes continued well into that century.

French-Canadian-made, nineteenth century washstands (70) show considerable originality and creativity, and appear to represent an expression of freedom and flamboyance! Generally, nineteenth century *armoire* doors were no longer embellished with lozenges, diamond points, scrolls, and carved fruit and flower designs as in the previous century. Doors made soon after the beginning of the nineteenth century usually closed flush with the stiles and rails of the containing structure or frame and no longer overlapped (lap doors) the frame as they did in the eighteenth-century types. The plain panels of the doors were generally raised (23) or sunken (inset) (24), with the raised panels more commonly in use at the beginning of the century. These gradually gave way to a dominance of sunken-panel types before the middle and during the latter part of the nineteenth century.

The evolutionary change from highly embellished doors of the eighteenth century to the less sophisticated, plain-panel types in the nineteenth century reflects the changing styles combined with the British and American influence on the French-Canadian joiner. Most importantly, the changes in style and construction also reflect the new socio-economic status of the humankind with the advent of the Industrial Revolution.

The introduction of New England and British (English, Scottish, and Irish) furniture styles and techniques of joinery to southern Quebec's Eastern Townships also appears to relate to the settlement pattern that developed in the region south of the St. Lawrence from Lévis westward to the higher country east of the Richelieu Lowland. The settlers of this vast wilderness were plain people: New England back-woodsmen, former British soldiers, farmers, tradesmen, and renegades. There were few urban, educated settlers among them. Their well-made, early country furniture reflects their simple, practical taste for the necessities of life.

While the Lake Champlain-Richelieu River passage served as the principle north-south route of commerce and settlement for nearly 200 years, it was not until shortly after 1790 that settlement took place in southern Quebec, south of the Seigneuries of the St. Lawrence River Valley and east of the Richelieu River Valley. Many of the settlers, being New Englanders, began their long journeys northward from the frontier towns of Claremont and Haverhill, New Hampshire, and Newbury, Vermont, via the

Connecticut River-Lake Memphremagog passage, settling in what is now Barnston, Coaticook, Hatley, Stanstead, and other adjacent communities in Quebec.[1] They brought some of their furnishings from New England with them. There is a label on a chest in the Brome County Historical Museum in Knowlton, Quebec, which reads "This chest is thought to have come from Newfane, Vermont, with some of the Knowltons between 1797 and 1821." The British discouraged settlement, wishing to keep an unsettled buffer zone between the United States and British Canada. Nevertheless, a settled population of considerable density was established by 1800-1810. In fact, for a number of years, this area was the most densely settled part of the Eastern Townships.[2] The settlers had an economic orientation toward markets in the United States or in Montreal and Trois-Rivières. Limited stagecoach connections from Quebec through the Eastern Townships area to Vermont and Boston were in effect by early 1811.[3] Quebec City, lying to the northeast, was isolated from the developing Eastern Township areas. The Craig and Gosford Roads[4] were built sporadically over a number of years, beginning about 1806, to connect Quebec City with the Eastern Townships area and to give it the similar economic advantages as Trois-Rivières and Montreal experienced.

In the early days, these "roads" were merely cart paths, but they did open the way from Quebec to the Eastern Townships for trade and limited immigration. While some British immigrants used these roads to settle the back country, a great many immigrants continued up the St. Lawrence to Montreal and then to upper Canada (Ontario), where large-scale settlement was in progress. For additional information on the furniture styles made by these settlers, refer to Pain's *The Heritage of Upper Canadian Furniture*. It should also be noted that at about the same time, Irish and Scottish immigrants traveled via the Nicolet River to reach the Eastern Townships area.

Some Americans followed still another route. They came down the Richelieu and St. Lawrence Rivers and then continued upstream along the St. Francis to the Ulverton-Richmond-Danville area, where they settled (circa 1805-1810).[5] Closer look at the early tombstones found in many cemeteries situated in the Eastern Townships from Stanstead to Ulverton and Kingsey Falls reveals almost exclusively American and British (English language) names. The changes in population that took place later in the nineteenth century are from the Census of Canada. According to *The Seventh Census of Canada*, 1931, pg. 149, the estimated population of Quebec (Lower Canada) in 1837 was 434,000 Frennch and 166,000 English (British). Some of this large pool of French-Canadians gradually moved southward into the Townships from the St. Lawrence Region, especially after the construction of the Arthabaska Road. Yet in the Eastern Townships, the majority population as late as mid-century was still English descent. For example, by 1861, the population of Richmond County in the heart of the Eastern Township was 8,844; 1,312 were of French descent and 7,532 were of British descent. The French-Canadians were still largely concentrated in the Seigneuries to the north in 1860, but they had begun to move into the Eastern Townships during the second quarter of the nineteenth century. The first French-Canadians arrived in Lennoxville in 1851,[6] and a large population was established by the end of the nineteenth century. Today, the adjacent city of Sherbrooke is about 90% French-Canadian.

It follows then that as the French-Canadians moved into areas formerly populated by New Englanders and scattered pockets of British immigrants, they brought with them their customs and techniques of furniture making. When they became aware of New England (American) and British country furniture styles and techniques of joinery, they apparently copied or modified these forms sometimes to suit their tastes, with an interesting mix the result. For example, many of the country work tables, or tavern tables as they are frequently called by New Englanders, were made in the old French or Continental manner by using flat, gently tapered, dovetailed-shaped incised cleats (figure 73) on the underside of the tops to keep them from curling. New Englanders most frequently cleated the tops of their work or tavern tables on the ends in the "breadboard top" fashion to keep them from curling. Otherwise, many are so similar to New England-made tables that it would be difficult to tell them apart. The frame construction in some cases, however, seems to be heavier and sturdier in pieces made by the French-Canadians. Sturdy cupboards made by French-Canadians during the earlier half of the nineteenth century often show the post-and-frame method of construction, a carry-over from Continental forms and French-Canadian joinery of the preceding two centuries. This method of construction was almost entirely given up in New England after 1725.

Footnotes

[1] John Lawrence, *The History of Stanstead County P.Q., Montreal, 1874*, pp. 2, 5.

[2] Anna E. Hoekstra and W. Gillies Ross, "The Craig and Gosford Roads: Early Colonization Routes in the Eastern Townships of Quebec," *Canadian Geographical Journal*, 1969. 79(2): pp. 52-57.

[3] *Annals of Richmond County and Vicinity*, Vol. 1, pp. 28-30.

[4] *Ibid*.

[5] Leslie L. Healy, "Hardships of the Early Pioneers of Richmond Tonwship (Que.), *Sherbrooke Daily Record*, March 14, 1953.

[6] Kathleen H. Atto et al, 1975, *Lennoxville (History of), Vol. 1*, p. 23.

# CHAPTER THREE

# The Identity Crisis

Many reputable dealers, to their credit, are very careful to identify accurately the origin of a piece before they sell it. In fact, they are often quite proud to say that this is a fine oak dresser from Leominster in England or a Hudson River Valley Kas from New Paltz, etc. Pieces with a long family pedigree from old-line, east coast homes are particularly desirable and often fully documented. But at the large, drive-in antique markets, such as in Brimfield, Massachusetts, an identity crisis has developed insofar as provenance is concerned. There, dealers by the hundreds are lined up next to each other from diverse locations across the United States and Canada and the goods rapidly pass hands once the selling and buying begin. By the end of two or three days, a piece could change hands several times. A table, for example, from Hermann, Missouri, could wind up in the hands of a New Hampshire dealer and then be sold as "a fine, old country piece," with nothing said about the provenance. The unsuspecting buyer would be none the wiser, but, spurred on by curiosity or perhaps by accident, might eventually learn the true provenance of the table, perhaps to his or her disappointment or delight.

Antique furniture and folk art from Quebec have been quite well-represented at Brimfield in the recent past. Unfortunately, American dealers do not always represent it as Canadian. The dealer, unfamiliar with its Canadian earmarks or unsure of its place of origin, sometimes sells it merely as country furniture.

"It was sold to me by a picker, but I don't know where it was made," is often the truthful answer one gets when asked about the provenance. However, it is not too unusual for some pieces with telltale Canadian characteristics to be sold to the uninitiated as coming from northern New England, upstate New York, or from way down the coast of Maine. In addition, some pieces may have been made in the border states years ago by a Canadian immigrant who continued to use the style and technique of joinery that he learned in his homeland. In years past, the seller may not have mentioned the Canadian provenance because the piece would have sold better with an implied American origin.

This does not seem to be so much the case today. Antique and quite old cupboards and tables are now in particularly good demand regardless of their origin. Country antique and near-antique furniture and accessories arriving in container lots from Great Britain and Western Europe, from Sweden to Spain, are selling very well today because they possess some of the same qualities of unsophisticated charm and magnetism we have seen for years in our Canadian and American country pieces. However, all of this mixing has added to the growing confusion of identity or origin, and I hope that the text and illustrations in this book will clarify, if only a little, what it is in the make-up of a piece of country furniture that says "Quebec."

It is disturbing to witness the disruption of cultural continuity when a piece is transferred from one region of a country to another or from one country to another country with no feeling for provenance, maker, shop, style, or time of construction. The more we know about a piece, the more important it becomes as a contribution to our national and international tree of cultural history. The point is, the addition of a fine antique to one's collection is more than another beautiful object to enhance a room; rather, it honestly represents and preserves a facet in the level of cultural or taste achievement that prevailed at a given time in human history and which never again will occur.

# CHAPTER FOUR

# Identifying Characteristics

It would be naive to say that a given characteristic determines for certain whether a nineteenth century piece of country furniture or accessory originated in Quebec. There is always the exception, possibly occurring wherever the people of Quebec later settled and continued their styles and techniques of joinery, whether in New Brunswick, New England, New York, Missouri, Ontario, and so on. In other cases, a parallel development of furniture styles occurred independently hundreds of miles apart. Nevertheless, telltale signs or earmarks point out the direction of origin, either cultural, geographical, or both. For example, a yellow-pine slab or a hunt board standing on long legs could be appropriately attributed to Georgia or the Southeast. Southern furniture was generally constructed to allow for better ventilation. A punched-tin pie safe (a form of food locker) from Pennsylvania or Ohio also allowed for better ventilation. While antique food lockers occur rarely in Quebec, no great need for ventilation existed with the less humid summers of shorter duration, so the punched tin was omitted or perhaps never even considered.

Just as the yellow-pine slab points to the southeastern United States, other pieces exhibit characteristics of material, joinery, and style which point toward Quebec and the French, British, and American traditions found there. Nineteenth century woodworkers borrowed ideas and techniques from each other, occasionally resulting in some interesting forms. In some rural areas, a long cultural lag persisted, which means that some pieces continued to be made virtually unchanged over many years.

It should be remembered that Quebec was not always as French as it is today. Americans, followed by the Scots and the Irish, settled the middle St. Francis River Valley. Much of the gentle upland Appalachian region south of the St. Lawrence Valley was settled by the British. Many of the early non-French settlers of Quebec were assimilated gradually by the French culture through intermarriage and sheer numbers. The resulting cultural mix, often reflected in interesting furniture forms, adds to the intrigue and complexity of antique studies in Quebec, an area in need of extensive research.

In my study of nineteenth century country furniture and accessories from Quebec, I have noted stylistic and constructional features and materials characteristic of that area, though not necessarily totally restricted to it. They are summarized here and, in many cases, discussed in more detail in other sections of this book.

## SUMMARY OF SOME IDENTIFYING CHARACTERISTICS OF NINETEENTH CENTURY QUEBEC COUNTRY FURNITURE AND ACCESSORIES

*Constructional*
1. Wood
2. Hardware
3. Incised Cleats
4. Chamfering and Beading
5. Mortise-Tenon Construction and Doweling
6. Drawer Bottoms
7. Chair Seats
8. Chair Arms, Frames and Rockers
9. Moldings
10. Aprons and Skirts
11. Victorian Turned Table Legs
12. Overhang on Dome-Top Trunks
13. Posts of Cradles
14. Door Panels
15. Unusual Size

*Non-Constructional*
1. Printed Paper as Lining of Cupboards

*Constructional Characteristics*

**Wood**

Two North American species, Eastern white pine and butternut (white walnut), dominated the construction of *armoires*, two-piece cupboards, corner cupboards, and other cupboard forms during the first half of the nineteenth century. However, during the last half of the century, white ash also was used extensively for the same purposes. White and yellow birch, together with some rock maple, found wide use in the construction of tables, particularly for the aprons and legs. Table tops, usually consisting of several boards, were commonly of pine or butternut. The whittled chair rounds or rungs of *habitant* chairs are chiefly ash. The use of black cherry and rock maple in large case pieces seems limited in view of the scarcity of surviving examples. Basswood or American linden also was used to a limited extent for case pieces, most notably in the region adjacent to the United States. Occasionally, spruce and red pine were mixed with Eastern white pine and Eastern hemlock for use in the construction of cupboard backs, drawer bottoms, and other inconspicuous areas.

The widespread importation of paint-stripped pine furniture into the United States from Western Europe has occurred in recent years. Much of it is in the British country tradition (particularly Irish), often similar in construction, style, and form to that made in Quebec and Ontario. One can easily misidentify its provenance. Generally, those pieces made in Canada are of Eastern white pine and/or butternut, whereas those constructed of the Western European hard or Scotch pine (*Pinus sylvestricus*) or its ecotypes came from Britain or the Continent. The grain and color of the European hard pine looks like some North American hard pine, but the boards are commonly characterized by an abundance of closely spaced, hard, pitchy knots, seldom seen in the North American species selected for furniture making.

Wood identification may not always be the final answer to the geographical origin of some traditional pieces. Howard Pain[1] has pointed out that during the nineteenth century, Canada shipped quantities of lumber to Britain, some of which was used for drawer parts, backs and carcasses of cupboards, and other purposes. In 1985 at a Michigan antique shop, we came across a number of large cupboards, recently arrived from Britain, which had all the earmarks of Eastern white pine. Without doubt during the nineteenth century, Canada provided Britain with large quantities of lumber, considerable amounts of which subsequently were used in furniture construction. It appears that some of this furniture is now arriving in North America as antiques. The serious students of antique furniture seeking additional knowledge about wood types might avail themselves of a college or university wood-identification course.

The stock for making the bodies, frames, and backs of Quebec country furniture was commonly 1" to 1⅜" in thickness. Sometimes the backing boards of *armoires* exceed two feet in width. Their unfinished outside surfaces quite often show the impression of a broad axe or an adze, especially in eighteenth and early nineteenth century examples. In others, up-and-down saw or (after circa 1840) circular saw marks usually are found on the backs. Framed panel backing of considerable merit is encountered on some of the better-made, early nineteenth century examples. The rectangular or square corner posts of *armoires* usually range from 2" to 4" on a side.

Post-and-frame construction of European ancestry and dating back to medieval times or earlier is characteristic of French-Canadian coffers, cupboards, and related forms of the 17th, 18th, and early 19th century.

**Hardware**

The wrought iron hinges found on the lap doors of *armoires* and other cupboards lend an appealing air to many early nineteenth century pieces. Perhaps the best known to the layman and a carry over from the eighteenth to the early nineteenth century are the rat tail or devil tail fische hinges. Widely used in Quebec and also in Pennsylvania, they attest to a common Continental-European origin. We have seen them used in Norway, France, and the Rhine River area in southern Germany. They were rarely used in New England, nor are they much at home on British pieces.

While fische (fiche) hinges, often without rat tails, were used quite commonly in Quebec on early nineteenth century lap-door cupboards, the changing styles and ongoing use of flush door cupboards throughout the nineteenth century prompted the use of cast iron butt hinges and, less commonly in the early part of the nineteenth century, "H" hinges. A very common practice from the outset was to mount the butt hinges on furniture with the faces or plates exposed, one-half mounted on the door stile and the other half mounted on the frame or body. This practice is almost a trademark saying "made in Quebec," although on occasion, I have seen examples from New Brunswick, New England, Virginia, Georgia, and other locations.

Plain chest or coffer hinges, including the offset variety, are well-represented in Quebec and similar to New England and British types. Probably Great Britain manufactured many.

The better-made latches and bolts are attached to escutcheons ornamented with scalloped edges, frequently terminating in a *fleur-de-lys* or similar trefoil ornamentation.

Characteristically French, long strap hinges appear on some large cupboard doors. They are mounted at one end on a pintle and terminate distally in an open heart-like form. To produce the heart, the smith expanded and split the hinge into two, in-curved, tendril-like strips of iron.

Another hinge form seen on some Quebec cupboards terminates in an expanded fish tail. However, fish tail hinges are not totally restricted to Quebec, although their forging and use there appears to have continued at a later date than in the United States.

The use of wrought iron nails also appears to have continued well into the second quarter of the nineteenth century, considerably later than in the United States. It is noteworthy that much of the iron forged in Quebec prior to and during the nineteenth century came from deposits found along the St. Maurice River Valley, a few miles northwest of Trois-Rivières.

Also of interest and quite distinctive because of their form are the stove and fireplace pokers made in Quebec. It is the variety of hand-forged "serpent head" hooks which make up the tips of the pokers that is so intriguing (figure 214).

## Incised Cleats

Flat and thin, gently tapered, incised, dovetailed-shaped cleats (keys) were used extensively to prevent curling on eighteenth and nineteenth century Quebec furniture. This method of construction, a carry over from Continental Europe, is seen frequently on the underside of worktable tops, the inside of the flat lids of coffers or storage boxes, the inside of non-paneled cupboard doors (figure 32), and also in other, wide-board construction pieces. The Mennonites and Doukhobors in Western Canada also utilized this kind of cleat in furniture construction.

On the other hand, in Pennsylvania, New York, and particularly New England, nailed or screwed board cleats applied to flat board surfaces were the order of the day on closet, cupboard, and house doors. Screwed, nailed, or wooden-pegged cleats also were applied to the ends of the tops of worktables or tavern tables in the so-called "breadboard" manner.

Some Pennsylvanian blanket and dower chests exhibit open mortise-and-tenon construction in the end cleats of the lids, which is an ingenious way to prevent curling. I have not encountered this in the

Quebec chests that I have examined. Wide-board, shaped end cleats, dovetailed to the underside of table tops and fitted snugly against the end skirts of the table frame, were used extensively in Pennsylvania, parts of Ohio, and Ontario, but seldom are they found in Quebec.

## Chamfering and Beading

The legs of chairs and benches and the stiles and rails of *armoires*, other cupboards, and chests of drawers commonly were chamfered or beveled. Chamfering also exists on the bodies of some other furniture pieces of post-and-frame construction, as well as on drying frames, towel racks, and so on. Some table legs are boldly and neatly chamfered only on the inside corner of each leg, from near the top to the extremity. More commonly, the square legs of many tables are handsomely chamfered on all four sides (figure 74). Chamfering gives furniture a degree of refinement and a feeling of lightness without which some pieces would seem very ordinary and cumbersome. The quality of chamfering found on many examples is of the highest magnitude and when combined with other features described in this section of the text, they clearly give a feeling of a Quebec origin.

The outside corners of many late eighteenth and early nineteenth century table legs are beaded (figure 75), tending to "dress up" everyday forms. Some tables treated in this manner might be called "country Chippendale." The origin of this refinement may be Anglo-American, although some early French-Canadian *armoires* are found with beaded posts.

## Mortise-Tenon Construction and Doweling

Open mortise and exposed tenon construction or joinery characterize chairs, and "H" and box stretcher-base tables made by Québécois working with square and rectangular wood stock. Chairs made by French-Canadians in the Côte de Beaupré and Ile d' Orleáans areas exemplify this type of construction.

Stretchers or rungs and seat rails commonly are doweled through the square legs of the various kinds of *habitant* chairs. The better-made examples show seat rails and bottom rungs held in place by wooden pins. The open mortise and exposed tenon construction, together with the doweled-through chair rungs and seat rails, all of native wood, serve as a clue to a Quebec origin with a British and French-Continental ancestry.

Very possibly some of the large, unrefined stretcher-base tables found in Quebec were made by

British immigrants following the British eighteenth and early nineteenth century folk tradition.

## Drawer Bottoms

The bottoms of the small drawers of many early nineteenth century Quebec tavern tables and work tables differ from many of those found in the United States in that the grain of the bottom board runs from front to back. This method of construction is a carry over from Britain and the Continent. Many of the American-made drawers, particularly those made by New England joiners, were constructed with the grain of the drawer bottom running at right angles to the drawer sides. It is quite common to find in the French-Quebec examples that the sides of small drawers are shouldered, butted, and nailed, both front and back, although dovetailed examples show up occasionally. It is often the case with Quebec tables that the drawers are narrow and deep, whereas New England work- or tavern-table drawers are commonly very wide.

## Chair Seats

Chair seats are of two major types: (1) solid wooden seats made from either thin boards or thick planks, and (2) those made of woven or stretched materials. The chairs with thin seat boards held to the frame with wooden pins or pegs date back to the seventeenth century and continued to be made in French-Canada into the early nineteenth century. These very distinctive chairs from around Quebec City, Ile d'Orléans, and the Côte de Beaupré are called Ile d'Orléans chairs (figure 98).

The seats of board or plank seat chairs usually are shaped from 2" thick to 3" thick stock. They include forms commonly found in America, such as five, six, and seven spindle and bird cage Windsors; half-spindle chairs, usually with three or four spindles; full, four spindle, rabbit ear chairs; and Boston rocker types of great variety.

The woven materials used in chair seating include rush (à la Capucine), split ash or elm bark strips, and rawhide thongs (often in a snowshoe weave) (figure 106). Stretched animal hide, not unlike that seen in some chairs from the American Southwest, commonly was used when nothing else was available. Replacement seats often are made of twisted yarn, heavy twine, plastic braid, or strips of rubber from inner tubes.

## Chair Arms, Frames, and Rockers

Certain nineteenth century, country hand-crafted chairs and settees or benches exhibit peculiarities of construction that arouse one's suspicion that they are from Quebec. For example, the thin arms on many of these chairs and certain benches exhibit a decided downward slope from back to front (figure 125), seldom seen in American chairs. The arms of woven seat chairs are supported up front by a continuation of the front leg or post above the seat rail as in American chairs. However, in some Quebec rocking chairs, the extension above the seat rail curves or is shaped laterally and upwardly in rib-like fashion to join the arm. This feature, with few exceptions, is not encountered in our antique, nineteenth century, country rocking chairs. Each rear leg extends upwardly as a part of the chair back above the seat rail and is shaped from one piece of wood. Beginning at the seat rail, the extension of each rear leg sweeps gently backward and upward to form the chair's back frame (figure 128), housing the crest and slats or splats. The backward curvature is typical of Quebec rockers.

The rockers attached to the legs of many antique chairs are held firmly in place by a nut and bolt. While this method of attachment is found on many chairs we see nowadays in Quebec, I suspect that, in many cases, the original rockers were held by wooden pins or nails. The use of the nut and bolt in this manner is characteristic of this region and, to my knowledge, was not a common practice south of the border.

The enormous rockers found on some cradles and chairs, ranging up to 3½" to 4" in thickness, also are characteristically from Quebec. In addition, their upper surfaces are sometimes attractively scrolled.

## Moldings

Moldings were widely used to "dress up" furniture made in Quebec and the United States. The liberal use and positioning of moldings gives us a clue to some Quebec-made pine and butternut furniture. For example, a narrow strip of molding sometimes was applied to ornate the lower outside edge of the aprons of tables and stands (figure 90). Other moldings were used to break up large surfaces, as was the case when a narrow strip of molding was tastefully situated on the surface (frieze) between the top or cap molding of a pine or butternut *armoire* and the tops of the *armoire* doors (figure 22). The molding usually was carried around the sides too. Occasional utilization of molding in this manner on early nineteenth century *armoires* may represent a neoclassical element. At a later date in the United States and Canada, similarly positioned moldings, as well as other moldings, were used extensively on mass-produced black-walnut and ash wardrobes.

Narrow strips of molding also were applied to the

surfaces of some large eighteenth and nineteenth century coffers or chests, as in the case of the Quebec "V" chests (figure 2). On some occasions, lozenges made from narrow strips of molding were applied to the top and/or sides of nineteenth century lift-top chests, the doors and sides of *armoires*, and other furniture forms, in an attempt to emulate the beautifully carved seventeenth and eighteenth century lozenge chests and other pieces of French-Canadian furniture. Antique furniture forms decorated with lozenges are not restricted to Quebec but are characteristic of that area.

A plain or beaded, thin, flat strip of wood (a fence) nailed to the four sides of the tops of some Quebec worktables produced a molded top. There was widespread practice of this technique in several parts of Quebec.

The process of applying flat strips of molding to the sides of a drawer is called "cocked-beading." This technique was widely used on Quebec-made, Empire and Victorian style furniture.

Quite often drawer fronts were ornamented by adding flat strips of molding about ½" to 1" wide to all four sides, producing a sunken-panel effect. Similar moldings were applied to the doors and sides of many cupboards.

Ornamentation took another form during the late years of the last century and early twentieth century. The widespread practice then was to frame or margin the doors, drawers, and sides of cupboards of all descriptions with thin, flat, cutout strips of wood . The cutouts commonly took the form of coarse saw teeth, lunettes, scrolls, dentils, and other forms, resulting in some grotesque examples. By now, the good taste and fine tradition of furniture making was nearly exhausted.

In many instances, moldings were nailed to the sides (stiles and rails) of sunken panels on various furniture forms. This was the customary practice in Europe, the United States, and Canada during the nineteenth century, and while it can be a broad guide to nineteenth century dating, it is of little use regarding provenance, in most cases. Moldings of the eighteenth century and earlier usually were shaped or cut into the surrounding stiles and rails of panels, becoming an integral part of them.

We also should remember that there was extensive use of heavy base molding on many post-and-frame case pieces and storage boxes from the seventeenth century to the mid-nineteenth century (figure 12).

The top or cap molding of nineteenth century *armoires* and other cupboard forms generally consisted of one or more applied, shaped moldings,

neatly fitted and nailed, whereas the cap molding used during the preceding two centuries on similar pieces often was cut from the thick, solid board top.

A continuous, narrow strip of concave or flat and grooved molding surrounding the fronts and sometimes the sides of the various cupboard forms is seen quite often on Quebec examples (figures 36 and 60). This ancient technique continued to be used into the nineteenth century.

**Aprons or Skirts**

The aprons or skirts found at the base of some nineteenth century country *armoires* and other cupboard forms are handsomely and distinctively shaped in a bold manner, contributing to the wholeness and balance of each piece. They were either cut out separately and applied to the base or shaped directly from the bottom rails. The bottom edges of the plank-ends of some case furniture also are attractively scrolled in the Quebec manner. Many follow along the Chippendale or Hepplewhite lineage, introduced to Canada by the British and Americans and then, in many cases, modified by the French-Canadians with a flamboyance that often says "Quebec." See Plate 1 tracing the evolution of aprons.

**Victorian Turned Table Legs**

Nineteenth century wood turners took their cue from much earlier times in making long tables for the church, farm, home kitchen, and other work areas. Many are of the large dimensions of seventeenth and eighteenth century refectory tables, but their legs most likely are turned in the Empire or Victorian style. One cannot help but admire the wood turner's ingenuity in producing such a variety of deeply turned legs as are found in Quebec. In some cases, blocks of wood, upwards of 6" on a face, were utilized. The desire on the part of the wood turner to express his personal taste and creativity seems unlimited. See Plate 2, illustrating some examples.

**Overhang on Dome-Top Trunks**

The thin topping boards capping the lids of many gently domed trunks or boxes (*coffres*) overlap all four sides by about a ½" on a side (figure 12). This often is seen in Continental forms, too, but is not characteristic of the Anglo-American country tradition. The Quebec examples, some dating to the seventeenth century, usually are painted rather than leather bound, like so many of the American small dome-top boxes.

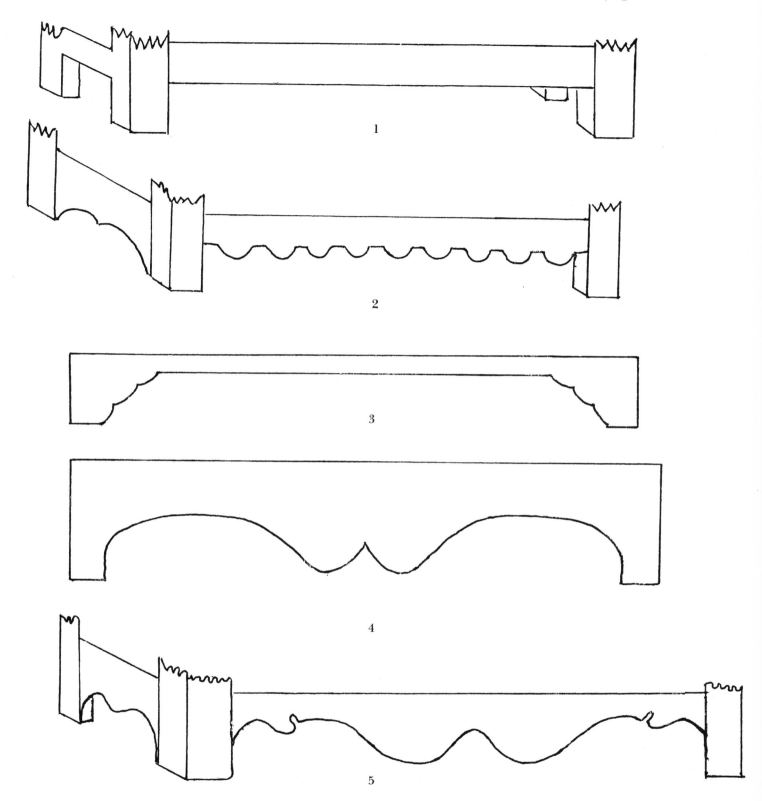

Plate 1. These drawings illustrate the range of form seen in the aprons or skirts of 19th century *Armoires* and related furniture. Numbers 1, 2, and 5 are a part of the bottom rail, the others are shaped and applied aprons.

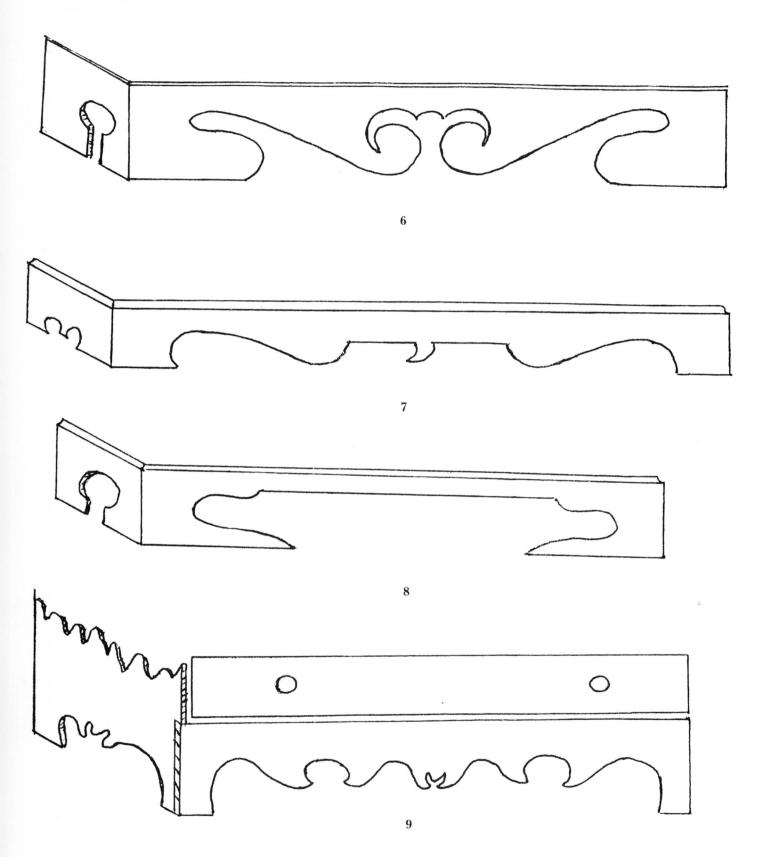

6

7

8

9

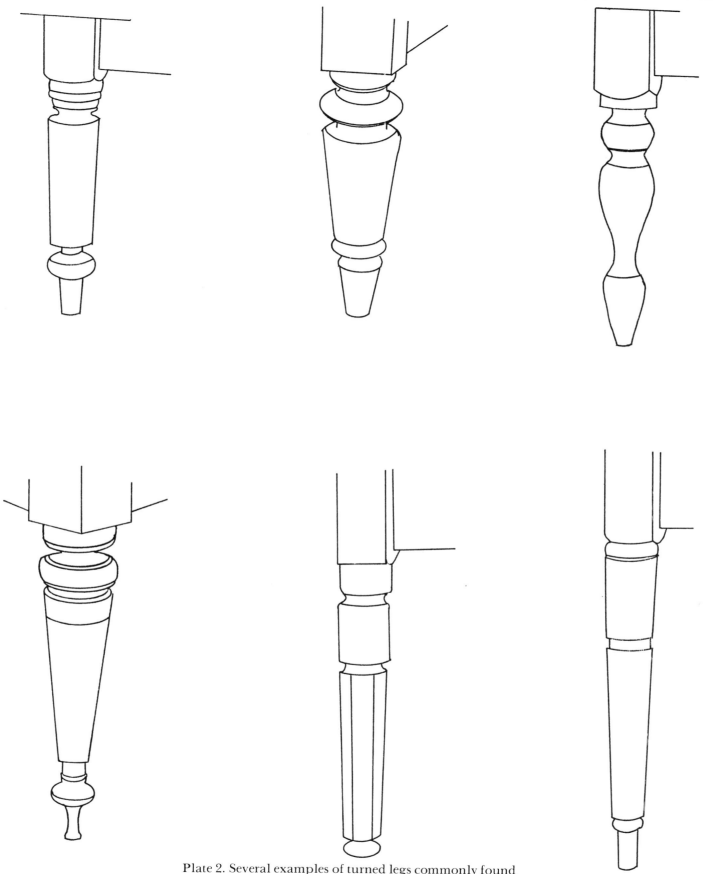

Plate 2. Several examples of turned legs commonly found on Quebec tables and stands, circa 1840-1880.

## Posts of Cradles

The four, extended and canted corner posts of Quebec eighteenth and nineteenth century cradles, rising from several inches to more than a foot above the side boards or rails, are a very distinctive feature (figure 152). At the other end, the corner posts of many cradles, particularly from the lower St. Lawrence Valley region, rest on very thick, boldly curved rockers that, it seems, were made to last forever.

## Door Panels

The changes occurring in the plain-type door panels of the various forms of nineteenth century case furniture may help in their relative dating.

Raised and beveled panels whose outside surfaces rise slightly higher than the surrounding thumbnail molded and slotted stiles and rails, usually date from the eighteenth or early nineteenth century, but probably no later than circa 1830. On the inside, these raised panels may be either flat (not rising as high as the stiles and rails) or thick (being flush to or rising slightly higher than the surrounding stiles and rails.) Some are beveled, too.

The earliest nineteenth century sunken or inset panels were fitted into slotted stiles and rails that usually were not thumbnail molded. A narrow decorative strip of molding often was applied to the exterior surface of the panel along the stiles and rails. On the inside, the panels often were beveled and raised, thus retaining their thickness and strength.

Later, during the second and early third quarter of the nineteenth century, thin sunken or inset panels of uniform thinness were fitted to slotted door stiles and rails. Narrow strips of molding may or may not have been applied to the outside surface along the stiles and rails.

During approximately the last third of the nineteenth century, the effect of a sunken panel, as viewed from the outside, often was produced by nailing a flat board to the inside of the door frame. This was done in both factory-made and individually crafted pieces. Many examples of this sort of weak, flimsy construction can be found today.

While the foregoing comments on nineteenth century door panels should be recognized as a generalized chronology of their development, it must be remembered that exceptions always occur. Furthermore, there always were a few gentlemen of "the old school" who practiced the old ways of joinery well into the twentieth century.

## Unusual Size of Furniture Forms

It seems appropriate to make some mention of the large size seen in some Quebec pieces of country furniture. Being New Englanders and quite accustomed to rather small and refined pieces of cherry, maple, and native pine rural furniture, we were at first overwhelmed, if not swallowed up by, the largeness of many cupboard forms, tables, dough boxes, and other pieces as we walked between the rows of the Elliott sisters' extensive stock back in the 1950s and early 1960s.

We observed some step-back cupboards exceeding 7½ feet in height and more than 4½ feet in width. A depth of 24" at counter level was quite common. Counter height commonly ranged from three to four feet. While there were smaller examples too, it was the large ones that predominated. *Armoires* commonly averaged from 48" to 56" in width and about 80" in height. Many stretcher-base and drop-leaf tables ranged from 48" to 52" in width and were quite low to the floor, averaging about 28". It has seemed so strange to us that cupboard forms were so tall and tables and *habitant* chairs so low. Certainly a case of extremes.

## Non-Constructional

### Printed Paper as Linings of Cupboards

Rough, as found, Quebec furniture has been shipped to the United States for years and sold as American. If there is some question in the viewer's mind regarding the origin of a piece of this furniture, he or she might find the answer by looking on the underside of shelves and where shelves abut back and sides. Do not be surprised to find French newspaper and other paper fragments, used as lining, with Montreal, Trois Rivières, and Quebec-Lévis identity. We recently looked at a European container lot and found Swedish newspaper fragments on cupboard shelves.

Makers' labels or initials are rarely found, if ever, on country furniture, but occasionally, owner identity stickers or labels do appear, suggesting a locality or area from which a piece has come. However, they should not be interpreted as meaning the locality where the piece was made.

Footnote

[1] Howard Pain, *The Heritage of Upper Canadian Furniture*, p. 519.

CHAPTER FIVE

# Blanket and Other Storage Chests or Coffers

1. A typical post-and-frame construction, French-Canadian storage box, or coffer, in original dark blue-green paint. Early 19th century. h: 21¼" x w: 38" x d: 20½". *Courtesy of Frederick and Lynne Johansson.*

Storage boxes, chests, or coffers are among the oldest forms of furniture that have come down to us through the centuries. From such forms, *armoires* and chests of drawers are derived. Many large, French-Canadian-made storage boxes utilized the post-and-frame technique of construction, with the tenons mortised into the square corner posts and held firmly with wooden pins. This technique, dating back to medieval times or earlier, continued to be used in Quebec into the nineteenth century. The bottoms of the chests were often 6" to 8" off the floor, with the four solid corner posts (which also served as legs) giving more than adequate support. Tongue-and-groove construction was employed when necessary to use two boards for a side, lid, or the bottom. Use of a flat, incised, dovetailed-shaped cleat kept the lids and sides from curling. Long, forged iron strap hinges commonly were utilized on the inside of the lids. Handsome iron locks secured the tops. In some examples, application of a narrow

strip of molding around the two sides and front at about the level of the lock broke up the large chest's plainness. The decorative molding was brought down in a "V" shape to avoid the lock and has since given rise to the use of the term "a Quebec 'V' chest." (figure 2)

Heavy moldings were applied, in many instances to the outer surface of the front and two sides at the level of the bottom of the chest. The use of a heavy base molding dates back to a much earlier time and its use often is seen in other storage pieces, including *armoires* and low buffets.

I have seen some late examples of storage chests assembled by first running a slot the full length of the corner post on two sides, after which a thin wooden panel was forced into each slot and then pinned in place. After the four panels (two side and the front and back ones) and the bottom were assembled, the joiner usually applied decorative molding to the sides of the panels. The bottoms of these chests, like the earlier ones, commonly stood about 6" to 8" off the floor and were supported by the

2. A white-pine, post-and-frame construction Quebec "V" chest, or coffer. The end view of each of the two, flat incised cleats, used to keep the lid from curling, is visible at the top. Early 19th century. *Courtesy of a friend.*

3. Broad, flat moldings frame the front and two side panels of this coffer. Moldings used as framing date back to a much earlier time. Early 19th century. *Courtesy of a Friend.*

5. Interior view of the coffer in figure 4. showing detail. The till is missing.

4. A small, white-pine coffer or box with hinged lid. The post-and-frame construction is characteristically French-Quebec, inspired by earlier continental forms. Boxes of this form were made in Quebec from the 17th to early 19th century. h: 14¾" x w: 17½" x d: 12⅜". *From a private collection.*

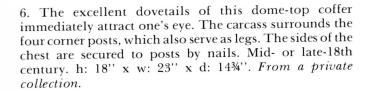

6. The excellent dovetails of this dome-top coffer immediately attract one's eye. The carcass surrounds the four corner posts, which also serve as legs. The sides of the chest are secured to posts by nails. Mid- or late-18th century. h: 18" x w: 23" x d: 14¾". *From a private collection.*

9. A dovetailed, pine coffer or blanket box, in original paint on small turned feet, possibly showing American influence. The lid is kept flat by a central incised cleat. Early 19th century. h: 21½" x w: 38" x d: 20¼". Courtesy of Peter and Monika Johansson.

7. An internal view of the coffer in figure 6. showing flat, dovetailed, incised cleats and corner posts. The sides are built around the corner posts and not mortised to them as is the more common practice.

8. A large, post-and-frame paneled coffer with cherry posts and ash framing; the top is a later replacement. Probably third quarter 19th century. h: 25¼" x w: 39¼" x d: 22¾". *Courtesy of Peter and Monika Johansson.*

10. A storage chest with molded and scrolled base, of probable Anglo-American influence. Early 19th century. *Courtesy of Cynthia Ballyntine.*

11. The overhanging top of this domed coffer or storage box illustrates a method of construction dating back to the 17th century or earlier. Early 19th century. h: 17½" x w: 30" x d: 19". *Courtesy of Jean Deshaies.*

12. A pine, dome-top, dovetailed chest or coffer. The ½" overhang of the molded lid is true to form. Other features making this a Quebec coffer include the positioning of the moldings and the feet. Late 18th or early 19th century. h: 13" x w: 23" x d: 13½". *Courtesy of Jennifer Mange, Historic Deerfield.*

four corner posts. Many pieces of post-and-frame furniture, as we see them today, stand much closer to the floor than when they were made because of wear and decay, caused by earthen floors and which necessitated the cutting back of the posts.

Not all of the large storage chests were constructed in the post-and-frame manner. There was also an abundance of six-board grain and blanket chests with the front, back, and sides butted and nailed or dovetailed. The plank end boards of those chests whose bottoms stood above the floor level were cut out in boot-jack or crescent form, just as in New England. Some of the large chests, mounted on stubby, turned feet or short, chamfered legs, are strikingly similar to rural chests found in the Mid-Atlantic States (figure 9). White pine and butternut usually were employed to make these chests during the early and middle nineteenth century, but as the supply of these woods diminished, increasing amounts of white ash were employed during the later years of the century.

14. A small Quebec white pine storage box in old black paint with typical exterior base molding. First quarter 19th century. h: 8½" x w: 17" x d: 11". *From a private collection.*

13. Small, raised-panel chests or coffers (*coffre à panneaux*) are not very common and generally highly prized by collectors. The post-and-frame construction is apparent. Early 19th century. h: 15" x w: 22½" x d: 13". *Courtesy of Jennifer Mange, Historic Deerfield.*

15. A small, white-pine box fitted with a pair of wrap-and-forged joint hinges. Late 18th or early 19th century. h: 11'' x w: 20'' x d: 12''. *From a private collection.*

16. Two small trinket boxes, the larger adorned with a lozenge and chip carving on the base molding, the smaller with a heart and diamonds. The fragment in the background is a ''rolling pin'' splash board from a *lave-mains*, or wash stand. Probably mid 19th century. Left: h: 4⅝'' x w: 12½'' x d: 6''; right: h: 3'' x w: 6½'' x d: 3⅜''; center: h: 10'' x w: 25''. *From a private collection.*

17. A small pine box made of Empire-style molding. Mid 19th century. *Courtesy of ''Decoy World.''*

# CHAPTER SIX

# Armoires

Many have always considered the well-designed, handcrafted, antique French-Canadian *armoire* to be among the most beautiful pieces of furniture produced in the New World. These rectilinear, one- or two-door cupboards, usually made of butternut or white pine, range in size from 2½ feet to 4½ feet in height in the petite *armoire* to 5 feet to 8 feet in height in the standard forms. Some medieval *armoires*, still extant in a few European churches and palaces, exceed 20 feet in height.

Similar forms, commonly made of ash, oak, cherry, basswood, pine, or black walnut, were made in the United States during the nineteenth century. The less sophisticated name of "wardrobe" was used for these pieces, often mass produced, particularly after 1850. The more sophisticated-sounding word *"armoire,"* derived from the French, means "a repository for arms." By the seventeenth and eighteenth centuries, they became commonplace and also were used for storing clothes and other items found in the home and church. Large eighteenth century cupboards or clothes presses made in the United States and of similar function as the French-Canadian *armoire* included the *kas* (Dutch) of the New York Hudson Valley area and New Jersey, and the *schrank* (German), which was made by Pennsylvanian Germans and their descendants.

The *kas* and the *schrank* usually were made in sections held by wedges. The large and heavy cornices can be dismantled from the body beneath, and the body can be lifted off the base unit containing the drawers. The front feet and sometimes the back feet, too, are large, turned, ball-shaped affairs. Regardless of the name and geography, these cupboards are, in reality, movable closets that were made to occupy large, open spaces situated along the walls of a home or an institutional building. Built-in closets are noticeably absent in many of the stone houses of Quebec, the Hudson and Delaware Valleys, and

18. A four-panel, single-door *armoire* in white pine. The base and hinges are quite recent additions. First quarter 19th century. h: 64" x w: 41½" x d: 18¼". *From a private collection.*

19. A small, plain, white-pine *armoire* with two removable, two-panel doors hung on fische hinges. Each side contains two similar panels. Late 18th or early 19th century. h: 55¾'' x w: 45¼'' x d: 15¾''. *From a private collection.*

20. The same as the *armoire* in figure 19. with one door removed. Details include post-and-frame construction, plain bottom rail without skirt, simple molded top, framed tongue-and-groove backing boards, and lightly molded outer frame (stiles and rails) on each door.

eastern Pennsylvania; therefore, the large cupboards served a very important function.

The French-Canadian country *armoire*, like its predecessor in rural western France, is of single-body (piece) construction. Four square or rectangular, heavy posts or stiles are used to frame the side panels and receive the top and bottom rails on the front and two sides. The backs of the early *armoires* also are paneled, but in most nineteenth century examples, they consist of tongue-and-groove, horizontal boards fitted to the two, rabbetted rear posts (figure 20). Until the early part of the nineteenth century, *armoire* doors opened and closed on either rat-tail or fische hinges, resulting in their lapping against the rails and stiles of the body (figure 19). Shortly after 1800, butt hinges were introduced and the doors hung on them fitted snugly into the rails and stiles. The lower rail, situated below the doors, is either plain or shaped. Some of the shaped, lower rails or skirts have a distinctively Québécois feeling (figure 36). It is not uncommon to find a bracket base in nineteenth century examples. In many of the earlier *armoires*, the heavily molded cornices exhibit a very pronounced overhang, usually balanced at the base by a heavy molding applied to the lower rail and extended along the two sides. The moldings of the nineteenth century *armoires* are generally lighter and nailed to the carcass or body.

Some *armoire* door panels and side panels found on the *armoires* of Quebec provide an interesting study in the evolution of design and style from the seventeenth to the early nineteenth century. The thick, white pine door panels of some seventeenth century *armoires* are carved to display multiple, deeply carved lozenges. During the eighteenth century, these diamond-shaped forms were more deeply carved and strongly beveled or faceted to produce high relief carvings called diamond points. Canadians and Americans alike today highly treasure the diamond-point *armoire*. Shaped door panels, often embellished with foliated scrolls reflecting the Louis XV style, made their appearance around the middle of the eighteenth century. *Armoires* built from about 1760 to 1790 often had the shaped doors, rails, and stiles embellished with floral carvings. The growing influence of Robert Adam and his associates is seen at the close of the eighteenth century and the beginning of the nineteenth century in the classical straight-line, geometrical forms that characterize the *armoire* of that time.

The English presence in Canada after 1760 is reflected in the chainging styles of furniture as more and more British woodworkers and cabinetmakers

Plate 3. This Quebec "V" chest or coffer, still retaining some of its old blue paint, clearly illustrates the post-and-frame construction so predominant in that province. *Courtesy of Musée de la Civilisation du Québec.*

Plate 5. A two-glazed-door, bow front, pine corner cupboard with two raised panel doors in the lower half; early 19th century. Note use of molding surrounding upper and lower halves of this piece. *Courtesy of Musée de la Civilisation du Québec.*

Plate 6. A very plain yet dignified single-glazed-door pine corner cupboard or cabinet; early 19th century. *Courtesy of Musée de la Civilisation du Québec.*

Plate 4. A post-and-frame, two-door, two-drawer early 19th century *armoire* in its original dark blue paint. This color is quite common on Quebec pieces. *From a private collection.*

entered the field. About 1800, a strong American presence and cultural influence took place in the Eastern Townships. The combined effect was gradually to Anglo-Americanize the country furniture of Quebec. *Armoires* made in the early nineteenth century lost their embellishments for the most part and the well-made, plain, raised panel *armoires* appear to have become the rule (figure 22). The arrangement of the panels varies considerably from two or three to three or four square or rectangular panels per door, with similar numbers of panels, in many cases, carried out on the two ends. Other *armoires* have one or two parallel, long panels in each door running from top rail to bottom rail (figure 34).

During the second and third quarters of the nineteenth century, sunken or hollow panels were commonplace in furniture forms. They were sometimes highlighted with narrow applied moldings or cutout and applied Gothic arches. In some examples, sawtooth or scrolled flat strips were used as moldings.

22. White-pine *armoire* with three graduated raised panels in each door. Each end has two panels of equal size. The front posts and rails and stiles of the body are beaded. An applied molding is found above doors and below cornice. First quarter 19th century. h: 71″ x w: 52½″ x d: 21½″. *Courtesy of Peter and Monika Johansson.*

23. Small pine *armoire* with three raised panels in each door. Sides unpaneled. First quarter 19th century. h: 73¼″ x w: 43¾″ x d: 14″. *From a private collection.*

21. White-pine, two-door, raised-panel cupboard or *armoire*. British influence is suggested by reeding surrounding each door and at top. This piece is probably the top of a two-tiered cupboard. Early 19th century. h: 56″ x w: 44½″ x d: 15½″. *Courtesy of Peter and Monika Johansson.*

24. Pine *armoire* with three sunken panels in each door and two similar panels on each end. Faint outline of a painted linen fold remains on each door panel. The exposed faces of the butt hinges are typical of Quebec. Second quarter 19th century. h: 68¼'' x w: 41¾'' x d: 17''. *From a private collection.*

25. *Armoires* of this form and beauty are scarce. Dating around 1800, this butternut and white-pine *armoire* combines French-Canadian and British elements. Note the Chippendale bracket base. Major restoration in the upper third. h: 80'' x w: 52½'' x d: 23¾''. *From a private collection.*

Plate 9. This 19th century tapered-leg table from the Musée de La Civilisation collection possibly is unique. Other tables with shaped, carved, and even pierced aprons do occur, but none probably exceed the beauty of this one. *Courtesy of Musée de la Civilisation du Québec.*

Plate 7. A butternut and pine hanging corner cupboard from the Montreal region; early 19th century. *From a private collection.*

Plate 8. A relatively plain, four-drawer pine commode from Saint-Gervais, Quebec, dating circa 1800. The feet, shaped skirt, rounded corner stiles, and three elliptical panels show a touch of the Louis XV style. *Courtesy of Musée de la Civilisation du Québec.*

Plate 10. A large Eastern Township rocking chair, still sporting much of its original mustard-yellow paint. Olive green, bright blue, and brick red were other favorite colors used for painting large pieces of furniture. *From a private collection.*

Plate 11. An early 19th century *habitant* arm chair with wings or headrests. The arms show characteristic sloping found on many Québécois chairs. *Courtesy of Musée de la Civilisation du Québec.*

Plate 13. This Empire bench bed or *banc lit* from the Musee De La Civilisation collection illustrates the intensity of color in the brick red paint used in Quebec. Provenance-Lanoraie, Quebec. *Courtesy of Musée de la Civilisation du Québec.*

Plate 12. This *habitant* chair illustrates how bright blue many country pieces were painted. Much of the original paint remains, with some restored. *From a private collection.*

Plate 14. A pine slant-top desk box on table; early 19th century. *Courtesy of Musée de la Civilisation du Québec.*

Similar changes exist in the two-tier and low buffets. In spite of the gradual loss of higher quality craftsmanship during the nineteenth century, *armoires* and other kin forms do retain their high utilitarian value and are widely sought today. The end of the line for the *armoire* was reached when board doors, butt hinges, and a butted-and-nailed, plain-board body were produced. The changes in style that evolved over so many years also are repeated in the two-tiered buffet *(buffet deux-corps)* and the low buffet *(buffet bas)*. Changes also are evident in the design of the doors of some of the later pieces, including hutches or dressers, corner cupboards, two-tiered glazed cupboards, and single-body glazed cupboards.

27. This low *armoire* or *buffet bas* in original old blue-green paint has two, single sunken panel doors and paneled ends. Hardware original. Two drawers are located at the bottom above base molding. Compare with figure 26. First quarter 19th century. h: 54'' x w: 48'' x d: 18¾''. *Courtesy of Peter and Monika Johansson.*

28. An all-pine, sunken-panel cupboard or linen press, incorporating two doors with sunken panels and a large, deep drawer at the base. The scrolled base is characteristically Quebec, but the overall form suggests Irish influence. Mid 19th century. h: 71¼'' x w: 54'' x d: 21''. *From a private collection.*

26. A small, white-pine, post-and-frame *armoire* with two drawers at top and two sunken or hollow panel doors below. Base molding is characteristic of many Quebec post-and-frame forms. Second quarter 19th century. The butt hinges are applied in the Québécois fashion. h: 61½'' x w: 41¾'' x d: 17¼''. *From a private collection.*

29. A small, flush-panel-door *armoire* in white-pine with two drawers at top. The single star-and-heart carving on each door may be unique to this piece. The front is framed with a molding characteristic of many Quebec pieces dating back to Louis XIII. Second quarter 19th century. *Courtesy of the Elliott sisters.*

30. A one-door pine *armoire*, possibly used originally as a bonnet cupboard. Hinges are a replacement. Early 19th century. h: 73'' x w: 34'' x d: 14½''. *Courtesy of Peter and Monika Johansson.*

Plate 16. Pail or bucket benches similar to this one were used in 19th century country homes throughout the province, usually occupying space near the sink in the dining area. *Courtesy of Musée de la Civilisation du Québec.*

Plate 15. A two-tiered early 19th century pine desk of the Anglo-American tradition. Book shelves are in back of the doors and four small drawers behind the fall front. *Courtesy of Musée de la Civilisation du Québec.*

Plate 17. The range of harmonizing color and size seen in 19th century pine storage boxes or coffers is well-illustrated by this grouping. *From a private collection.*

Plate 18. The second row of coffers clearly illustrates the post-and-frame construction so characteristic of much 18th- and 19th century Quebec furniture. *From a private collection.*

Plate 19. Hand-crafted 19th century *habitant* chairs, no two of which are alike. Note the subtle differences and residual paint. *From a private collection.*

32. A view of the *armoire* in figure 31. with the door removed, showing flat, dovetailed, incised cleats on the inside surface. This method of applying cleats was widely practiced in French Quebec. Printed paper fragments might give information regarding area of origin.

33. The simplicity of this two-board-door *armoire* or food storage cupboard is apparent. Cleats, as in the previous example (figure 32.), are found on the inside of the doors. Second quarter 19th century. *Courtesy of Brassworks.*

31. Simple, one-door Quebec *armoire* with fische hinges. The space at bottom is unusual. Top molding replaced. First quarter 19th century. h: 61'' x w: 27½'' x d: 15''. *From a private collection.*

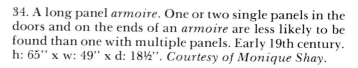

34. A long panel *armoire*. One or two single panels in the doors and on the ends of an *armoire* are less likely to be found than one with multiple panels. Early 19th century. h: 65" x w: 49" x d: 18½". *Courtesy of Monique Shay.*

36. This well-proportioned, raised panel *armoire* is very much a Quebec piece. The molding surrounding top and sides of the front, scalloped or festooned skirt, and molding on the center post entering the top and bottom rails are its strong points. Late 18th or early 19th century. h: 74½" x w: 57" x d: 19½". *Courtesy of Monique Shay.*

35. A small or petite *armoire* in original dark green paint. The placement of door panels, together with their surrounding rails and stiles, creates an interesting "cross" effect. Probably second quarter 19th century. h: 54" x w: 48" x d: 19". *Courtesy of Monique Shay.*

Plate 20. Some 85 pitchers and almost as many bowls tell us something about numbers of washstands that once populated the province. Besides pitchers and bowls, some 40 cradles and a grist of other items fill up this niche in the four-acre yard of the Elliott sisters. This is an August afternoon scene in 1960.

Plate 21. Another view of the Elliotts' back yard in August, 1960. Their 1830s Greek-Revival homestead provides background for an loading operation. Where do you suppose these antiques are today?

A number of old country houses are shown in Plates 22 to 26, to give the reader a better opportunity to visualize what the structures looked like where antiques, similar to those seen in this book, might have been used. However, as the twentieth century advanced, mass-produced furniture, pottery, glass, hardware, etc., replaced the old furniture and other old objects, which were then relegated to the barns and sheds. It was in some of these buildings that the pickers found their treasure troves in the 1950s and 1960s. See Plates 27-32.

Plate 22. An old stone farmhouse near Nicolet, Quebec. Its saltbox form suggests a New England type of building, but the chimneys built on the outside walls of the main structure give it a Québécois identity.

Plate 23. A small stone farmhouse located near St. Lambert as it appeared in 1967. It probably dates about 1800 and is rather typical of the smaller stone structures of the Montreal region.

Plate 24. A handsome late 17th or early 18th century farm home, typical of the Levis-Quebec-Ile d'Orleans region. Note the steep roof and truncated gable.

Plate 25. This brick cottage house with its casement windows and sweeping roof is a form quite typical of houses built during the 19th century in Quebec. Many others, like this one, were made with wooden exteriors.

Plate 26. Another early 19th century stone farmhouse, with later additions, not far from Chambly in the Montreal region. Note the large chimney, the small glass pane casement windows, and the stone corners (*coins*).

37. This uniquely carved, small pine *armoire* in the folk tradition remained the possession of one family for nearly 150 years before coming on the market in 1986. Central Chaudière River Valley, Quebec. h: 68'' x w: 48'' x d: 16½''. *Courtesy of Guy Boucher.*

# CHAPTER SEVEN

# One-Piece, Step-Back Cupboards and Hutches

38. A tall, one-piece step-back cupboard in painted pine, typical of the Quebec form. From St. Lawrence Valley near Rivière du Loup. h: 86" x w: 52" x d: 22". *Courtesy of Brian DuMoulin.*

One-piece, step-back cupboards (figures 38, 39, and 40) were made in large numbers in Quebec during the nineteenth century and could well represent the influence of American and British immigrants in French Canada. Step-back cupboards from Quebec commonly are made of thick stock, often 1" to 1⅜" in thickness. The cupboard counter surfaces are not uncommonly 3 feet high with the total height of the cupboard nearly 7 feet or even higher, some monstrous in their proportions. The face boards, sideboards, and backboards are butted and nailed, with the post-and-frame construction, commonly seen in French-Canadian *armoires*, generally absent. French-Canadians, no doubt, made many cupboards following the Anglo-American influence; however, they often took time to ornament them with heartfelt decorative creations.

The arrangement of cupboard doors varies considerably. Common placement of doors included 1-over-1, 2-over-1, 2-over-2, or 1-over-2; a few never had doors, and many have lost their doors over time. Door construction varied considerably. Some cupboard doors consist of plain boards with tapered, flat, incised, dovetail-shaped cleats set into them to prevent curling. Others consist of doors made of stiles and rails (mortise-and-tenon construction with wooden pins) surrounding a panel. Raised panels, commonly utilized in the earliest part of the nineteenth century, represent a carry over from late eighteenth century types. They gave way to flush and, more commonly, sunken or hollow panel construction during approximately the later two-thirds of the nineteenth century. Shaped panels seen in Louis XIV and XV forms disappeared completely by the time the step-back cupboard was in vogue.

An aesthetic quality was produced for an otherwise very plain panel door by applying narrow moldings to the sunken panel along the inner edges of the stiles and rails. The crown of the moldings rises slightly above the surround. Moldings applied to the door

Plate 27. A low, long barn typical of French Canada as seen in the Chaudière River Valley. Note the placement of windows.

Plate 30. An Anglo-American 19th century barn in southern Quebec. Early settlement here was by Americans followed by British, which resulted in a different early material culture than found in the St. Lawrence River Valley.

Plate 28. A long, two-door, thatched-roof barn near Pierreville as it appeared in 1965. There is copious space within for hay storage, threshing machines, animals, and cattle- and horse-drawn vehicles. Thatched roof barns are a dying breed today.

Plate 31. A small lean-to shed attached to barn in the New England manner, seen near Weedon-Centre, Quebec.

Plate 29. A very steep, thatched-roof hay barn of much earlier times, as seen near Saint-François du Lac in 1965.

Plate 32. These two connected barns, one for cattle and the other for hay, are quite typical of northern New England. This scene is near Coaticook in southern Quebec.

panels of *buffet à deux corps* produced a stunning effect, too. Eighteenth century stiles and rails on Canadian and American doors were usually thumbnail molded (cut out of the solid body of wood) on the exterior where they received the panel. This method of construction fell out of fashion in both areas by the early nineteenth century, when applied moldings took over. It is interesting to note that the architectural use of applied moldings on exterior and interior house doors, cupboard doors, chimney breasts, fireplace surrounds, ceilings, etc., was widespread during Federal, Neoclassical (Greek Revival), and Victorian times in both countries.

39. A four-door, step-back cupboard very characteristic of Quebec. The sunken or hollow panels with applied moldings and butt-hinged doors suggest a second quarter 19th century date. The heavy top molding represents 18th century influence. h: 78½" x w: 55 x d: 18¾". *Courtesy of Monique Shay.*

40. An early blue-painted, one-piece step-back cupboard, with several unusual features. They include the expanded counter to form a pie shelf, seen behind the oval cutout, the presence and positioning of the two small drawers, and the small half-round cubby door. Early 19th century. h: 81½" x w: 43" x d: 19½". *Courtesy of Monique Shay.*

41. Another step-back form is the open-dish dresser (*Vaisselier*). The back is a replacement, for when it was picked, the pickers tore it from the wall to which it had been nailed. The flat moldings and overall form suggest Irish influence. The hinges are of wrought iron. First third 19th century. h: 81½'' x w: 56'' x d: 18¼''. *From a private collection.*

42. A well-balanced, small, unsophisticated white-pine, open-dish dresser or hutch (*Vaisselier*). The dish rails are mortised through the end boards. Mid 19th century. h: 75'' x w: 50½'' x d: 19''. *Courtesy of Monique Shay.*

43. This large, pine dresser from Quebec, with its cut-outs in the frieze and interesting door and panel arrangement, suggests strong Irish influence. Early 19th century. h: 85½'' x w: 57¼'' x d: 23''. *Courtesy of Monique Shay.*

Another form of one-piece, step-back cupboard found in Quebec is the open hutch or dish dresser (figures 41, 42, and 43). It differs from the one-piece, flat-to-the-wall, enclosed step-back cupboards described above, which generally postdate the open dish dresser in their development. The area above the counter and between the end boards was designed to remain open, with several exposed shelves for display purposes. One might think of the open dish dresser, in terms of its evolution, as the half-way point between a plain wall-hung shelf rack and the enclosed step-back cupboard.

The side or end boards of many New England eighteenth century examples are scrolled above the counter surface, and occasionally this is seen on Quebec examples, possibly representing Anglo-American influence. For the most part, it was during the early nineteenth century that the open dish dresser acquired its enclosure above the counter surface. The facing enclosure, nailed to the two vertical end boards above the counter level, usually consists of a narrow, plain, beaded or molded strip of wood about 2'' to 3'' in width. Sometimes architecturally pleasing columns or pilasters were utilized in more formal examples. A plain, molded, or shaped board completed the enclosure at the top or frieze. While a cornice may or may not have been applied, French-Canadian joiners often used heavy cornices, in keeping with their tastes.

# CHAPTER EIGHT

# The Two-Tiered Buffet or Two-Part Cupboard

44. A white-pine, two-part, step-back cupboard in "as-found" condition. Moldings are applied against rails and stiles that surround the panels. The molded cornice is well-executed and carried out in lower half too. Anglo-American influence. Mid 19th century. *Courtesy of "Decoy World."*

A two-tiered buffet, *buffet deux-corps* (figures 44 and 45), also called a double-bodied armoire or two-part cupboard, consists of two cupboards with the smaller, upper one made to fit onto the larger, lower one. Three or four shelves are characteristic in the upper cupboard and two in the lower. The front and sides of the upper body are set back and set in, respectively, over the lower body and usually framed by a small molding to hold the body firm.

The upper and lower parts normally have two doors. The lap doors and sometimes the bodies of the seventeenth and eighteenth century post-and-frame examples are highly ornamented with various kinds of shaped panels or geometrical forms, such as lozenges; there is also extensive use of heavy molding. The flush doors of early nineteenth century pieces consist of stiles and rails surrounding either raised, flush, or sunken panels. In many of the mid- and late-nineteenth century cupboards, each door consists of a frame (rails and stiles) to which a thin board is nailed on the inside to produce a sunken panel. As viewed from the outside, sunken panels may be highlighted by nailing a narrow finish molding against the rail and stiles. In other cases, very thin board cutouts, such as Gothic arches or a denticulated or a sawtoothed board strip, ornament the door. The plain board sides of the cupboard frequently are treated the same way to create the effect of paneling. It is most likely that the garish paint that we see on some of these cupboards today was applied during the twentieth century. The cutouts often appear in one color, the panels in another, and the door frames in still another!

When drawers are used in the upper cupboard, they usually are found immediately below the doors, and in the lower cupboard, they are placed immediately below the counter and above the doors. The drawer fronts commonly overlap the body of the buffet. In many of the cupboards from Quebec, the counter surface is exceptionally high, often 3 feet to

45. A large, two-tiered ash storage cupboard, commonly found in Quebec. Probably third quarter 19th century. h: 84" x w: 48" x d: 19½". *Courtesy of "Decoy World."*

46. A two-part cupboard in ash, maple, and pine, with sunken case and door panels. The rounded corners, the base, and the counter indicate Victorian influence. Last third 19th century. h: 80" x w: 58" x d: 22½". *Courtesy of Monique Shay.*

3½ feet from the floor. Simple bracket feet with a plain or scrolled skirt support some of the better made, two-part cupboards; others rest on the floor without the benefit of feet. The top of the upper cupboard is usually finished with either an applied, heavy concave or convex molding. These cupboards bear a strong similarity to those of the British Cottage tradition, particularly some of those from Ireland that currently are arriving in North America in container lots.

Many crude, two-part cupboards of the mid- and late-nineteenth century consist of nothing more than butted and nailed, plain-board construction and board doors. The board doors usually are kept from curling by the use of a flat, incised, dovetailed cleat. There is minimal molding, or none at all, on many of the plain-board examples.

48. A two-tiered, step-back cupboard in solid bird's-eye maple reflecting Anglo-American influence. Note the quarter columns, dentils, and Victorian molding. Southern Eastern Townships, Quebec. Third quarter 19th century. *Courtesy of Rodney Lloyd.*

47. A two-part Empire ash cupboard. Interesting features include sunken-panel doors with applied molding, typically scrolled legs and two drawers over the two doors in the bottom half. Third quarter 19th century. h: 80" x w: 50" x d: 20". *Courtesy of "Decoy World."*

49. The older cupboard above with "H" hinges (first quarter 19th century) is placed on the later (second quarter 19th century) sunken- or hollow-panel low buffet or sideboard showing Anglo-American influence. The open-face butt hinges of the low buffet are characteristic of Quebec. Top: H: 45" x w: 41" x d: 13½"; Base: h: 32½" x w: 51½" x d: 18¼". *From a private collection.*

50. The heavily molded top and deeply set panes of glass are often seen in glazed cupboards from Quebec. Third quarter 19th century. h: 45" x w: 40½" x d: 14¾". *From a private collection.*

# CHAPTER NINE

# The Low Buffet *(Buffet Bas)*

The nineteenth century country *buffet bas*, or low buffet or cupboard, is a form usually wider than high and often used as a sideboard. The small, rectilinear types resembling *armoires* also are called a *buffet bas* in Quebec. The doors and sides of some examples consist of plain panels, either raised or sunken. Unlike many eighteenth-century examples (figure 51), they do not have rich detail or ornately shaped panels. There are usually from one to four drawers (one of which could be false) beneath the top or the work counter and situated above one to four lap or flush doors (figure 53). Less commonly, drawers are located beneath the doors and above the base molding. The body often is of post-and-frame construction, with the corner posts or stiles extending three to six inches below the frame's base to give the effect of standing on short legs. Continental construction of this kind carries over into the nineteenth century from a much earlier time. The eastern white pine or butternut *buffet bas* with corner posts is sufficiently distinctive in form and style to label it characteristically French-Canadian.

51. For sake of comparison, this one-drawer, one-door low buffet *(buffet bas)* or commode is shown. It is of white-pine and a characteristically French-Quebec piece with the correct hardware, lift-off door, and a heavy molded drawer and door. A St. Andrews cross is cut into each of the raised door panels. Top replaced. Early 18th century. *Courtesy of Guy Boucher.*

52. This late-18th century low buffet or *buffet bas* is the precursor of many two- and three-door 19th-century types. Late 18th century. *Courtesy of Guy Boucher.*

53. A three-door, three-drawer low buffet or sideboard. Note the manner in which the flush doors are mounted. Moldings are applied to door panels. While the overall form of this piece shows British influence, the molded frame surrounding the front has a Québécois feeling about it. Second quarter 19th century. *Courtesy of Cynthia Ballyntine.*

55. American Empire sideboard or *buffet bas* in butternut from Drummondville, Quebec. The case is dovetailed and the molded top is a single piece of butternut 21¼'' by 67½''. Flat strips of molding frame each drawer. h: 36'' x w: 68'' x d: 22¾''*From a private collection.*

54. A white-pine *buffet bas* or sideboard with sunken panel doors. The apron or skirt is characteristic to Quebec. The plank ends also are scrolled at the base. It would not be unusual to find a similar piece with a smaller, matching step-back cupboard resting on the base unit. Second or third quarter 19th century. h: 39½'' x w: 47¾'' x d: 21''. *From a private collection.*

Other nineteenth century low cupboards or buffets (figure 54) are of butted and nailed board construction, possibly representing the Anglo-American influence. They often stand on bracket feet with a plain or well-shaped skirt, or apron, below the doors. Still others showing American Empire influence are supported by either ogee or turned, bulbous feet, while a few rest directly on the floor without the advantage of feet (figure 55).

56. A Victorian, three-door sideboard in white ash. Cut-out and applied linen-fold panels ornate all three drawer fronts. Figures 53 through 56 illustrate some 19th century changes in this form. Last third, 19th century. h: 54½'' x w: 56'' x d: 19½''. *From a private collection.*

58. This late-Victorian low buffet or sideboard is representative of the changes in style and construction that took place by the close of the nineteenth century (see figures 52 and 55 for comparison). Principally ash mixed with basswood and butternut. h: 37'' x w: 45'' x d: 17''. *From a private collection.*

59. A one-piece, flat-front, painted pine glazed buffet or cupboard. This form, likely representing British influence in Quebec, is not encountered too often. Mid 19th century. *Courtesy of Jean Deshaies.*

57. Two matching doors from a low buffet, inside and outside views. The top rail of the frame of each door is cut out in Gothic fashion. The simple door panel on the left is nailed to the door frame, producing a sunken panel similar to the one seen on the right. This kind of construction is characteristic of the last third of the 19th century when good workmanship was on the decline. h: 24'' x w: 13½'' x d: 1¼''. *From a private collection.*

# CHAPTER TEN

# Corner Cupboards

Corner cupboards played an important role in the furnishing of Quebec country homes for more than a hundred years. Free-standing corner cupboards were particularly popular from the mid-eighteenth century until after the middle of the nineteenth. Just as French-Canadian *armoires* evolved during that period from quite sophisticated forms reflecting somewhat diluted continental French taste to much plainer types, the corner cupboard also changed, reflecting less French influence and the increasing Anglo-American presence as seen, particularly, in Adam or Federal styling. The late eighteenth century, shaped panel doors (Louis XV manner) gave way in the early part of the nineteenth century to doors with plain, rectangular, raised panels, and, still later, to sunken (inset) panels, often accented by applied moldings. While many corner cupboards of considerable diversity were built, fewer of them have survived than the *armoires*.

Corner cupboards consist of both one-piece and two-piece or two-tiered construction (figure 61). It is not unusual to find one or two cutlery drawers situated beneath the counter (if there is one) and above the bottom door or doors (figure 62). A variety of door arrangements exists in these cupboards, including 1-over-1, 2-over-2, and 1-over-2. Lap doors supported by rat-tail fische hinges are found on some pieces made in the early nineteenth century, but flush doors supported by either butt or "H" hinges are usually the case. The upper door or doors, usually glazed, have several panes in each door. A few cupboards, called open cupboards, never had an upper door or doors (figure 62). In some examples, the rail above the top door and the vertical side pieces or stiles, carved in the folk art manner, impart a particularly French-Canadian flair to the piece. The more sophisticated cupboards are crowned sometimes with ornate molding and dentils. Bow-front

60. The lap door mounted on fische hinges and the cornice suggest a Quebecois origin for this cupboard. However, the overall form, with a storage area at the base for pails and pots, could represent British influence. Early 19th century. h: 80" x w: 38" x d: 15". *Courtesy of Monique Shay.*

by a medial rail that intersects and crosses a medial stile (muntings). The result is a door with four panels (two upper, small panels and two lower, large panels). The definitive medial rail and medial stile, both of considerable relief, stand out as a cross. A door of this type is referred to sometimes as a "Christian door."

61. A butternut, two-part step-back corner cupboard found near the Canadian border in northern New Hampshire. A southern Quebec origin is strongly suspect because of its broad counter and deeply set back upper cabinet. Second quarter 19th century. h: 80" x w: 49" x d: 21½". *From a private collection.*

cupboards, although appearing in the eighteenth century, continued to be made in limited quantities in the early nineteenth century and also reflect the changes in style that occurred then. Some cupboards sit harshly flat on the floor without the benefit of feet or a decorative skirt, while a shaped skirt and bracket or French feet softened the appearance of others.

Less common than the standing corner cupboards are the hanging corner cupboards. Most of these have one door, either paneled or glazed. The door of a hanging wall cupboard in the author's collection (figure 64), besides being surrounded by the usual marginal rails and stiles, is given further definition

62. A plain, open-top corner cupboard in the old paint with a cutlery drawer and two sunken-panel doors. The molding at the top and applied moldings on the doors probably date this piece mid-19th century or slightly earlier. h: 82" x w: 53" x d: 25". *Courtesy of Monique Shay.*

63. This simple form of pine corner cupboard can be found in New England and Quebec. The applied moldings visible in the upper half are characteristic of many Quebec pieces. Early 19th century. h: 72⅞" x w: 29" x d: 20". *Courtesy of Jennifer Mange, Historic Deerfield.*

64. A hanging corner cupboard in butternut and pine. The beauty of this cupboard lies in its "Christian" door. First quarter 19th century. h: 43¼" x w: 31¼" x d: 18". *From the author's collection.*

# CHAPTER ELEVEN

# Chests of Drawers or Commodes

A chest of drawers is a commode to the French-speaking world. While Quebec produced many commodes, the sophisticated pieces were made in the larger cities for a growing *bourgeois* clientele. The earlier pieces often reflect French influence, particularly of the Louies, and one can trace the stylistic changes in them just as in the *armoires*. They, too, were derived from coffers or storage chests. At the beginning, one drawer was added to the base of a storage chest, and by the process of addition, evolved at a later date to the two-drawer chest, and so on, ultimately resulting in a chest of three or more drawers. In neighboring New England, the evolution from storage chest or blanket box to a one-drawer, two-drawer, and multi-drawer blanket chest (a chest of drawers) likewise is easily traceable.

The more sophisticated pieces appearing by the beginning of the nineteenth century, notably of the Chippendale, Hepplewhite, Sheraton, and Regency styles, demonstrated strong British and/or American influence. Many of the more attractive examples have found their way to private and museum collections and seldom went on the market. Montreal and Quebec City sources also provided Canadian-made period mahogany chests, candle stands, and other important pieces for the New England and New York antique markets as early as the 1920s, and their Canadian origin soon was lost south of the border. The real interest in Canadian country antiques by Canadians and Americans, with few exceptions, did not blossom until the 1950s.

Nineteenth century country commodes usually are made of pine, birch, or butternut, with some of the later ones made of black walnut or ash. Some chests show no particular affinity to style. However, others, while retaining an interesting Québécois flair, clearly demonstrate such an affinity, notably, to the American Empire and Victorian.

Many of those pieces made in the latter part of the nineteenth century were factory manufactured and were parts of a set of furniture. However, it is not the intent of this book to go into a description of mass-produced cottage or formal black-walnut furniture found in Canada, which is virtually identical to American pieces.

Early nineteenth century commodes were never as abundant as the early chairs, tables, storage boxes, cradles, flax wheels, *armoires*, churns and dough boxes that we encountered at the Elliott's during the 1950s. However, there were numerous Empire forms, dating from about the middle of the nineteenth century, showing an abundance of ogee curves, and half and full columns and spindles.

The early nineteenth-century Québécois country commode, quite low, wide, and deep, usually consisted of three drawers . The drawers have tremendous storage capacity, each normally separated from the other by a dust board. The plank ends of these chests often show Québécois-style scrolling at the base, with the apron beneath the bottom drawer scrolled in the same manner (figure 65). The tops are framed in the Continental style, with a surround consisting of flat boards about 2½'' to 3'' in width, extending across the front and along each side and the back. They are joined at each corner by a miter joint.

Cocked-beading characterizes many drawer fronts of the early nineteenth-century commodes as well as the later Canadian-made Empire forms, circa 1850. The early British and Regency styles most likely lent the idea of cocked-beading. While the drawers of New England country chests occasionally are cocked-beaded, notably in some Hepplewhite and Sheraton (Federal) examples, generally cocked-beading was not used so extensively as in Quebec. Cocked-beaded drawers, however, are widely represented in Eastern and Central Pennsylvania.

The American-Empire furniture of New England and New York state no doubt strongly influenced the work of furniture makers in Quebec. As a result, the

65. The shaped apron and overall proportions of this butternut and black walnut chest of drawers or commode spell out its French-Canadian origin. The top surface is surrounded on all four sides by wide, flat, molded trim in the Continental manner. Early 19th century. h: 35" x w: 47" x d: 21¾". *From a private collection.*

66. The overhang of the upper bank of drawers, ogee scrolled feet and columns, and overall heavy proportions make for a classic Empire-style, white-ash bonnet chest. Mid or late 19th century. h: 49½" x w: 50" x d: 22". *Courtesy of Guy Boucher.*

67. A typical, small bonnet chest or commode with a deep drawer on each side, flanking two medial small drawers. There are three large drawers below, as shown here. The number of small, medial drawers near the top commonly range from two to five. The apron is a form true of many Quebec chests. Mid 19th century. *Courtesy of Cynthia Ballyntine.*

low, squat commodes of the early nineteenth century grew taller by adding more drawers (all enclosed within the enlarged case) above the basic three-drawer unit. These additional drawers collectively make up the overhang so characteristic of Empire chests. Supporting columns appear to each side of the drawers from beneath the overhang to the scrolled or deeply turned feet at the base. The supporting columns were scrolled in the ogee manner or turned on the lathe and, frequently, split and applied to the case. In some examples, the split columns are discontinuous, extending only part of the way down the front in pendant-like fashion. The turnings range in style from that of late-Sheraton to Victorian spooling.

Quebec has both individually crafted and factory-manufactured Empire pieces. Some of the joiner-made chests have plank ends with attractive scrolling at the base and a characteristically Québécois scrolled apron across the front. The front feet, formed from the union of the apron and end boards, vaguely resemble the French feet of the Hepplewhite style.

The number of drawers found in the overhang above the basic three drawers varies from one to six or more. Those with two large, rectangular drawers, one to the left and one to the right, and several small, tiered drawers situated between them are popularly called "bonnet chests". Nearly all are adorned with supporting columns of some kind (figure 66), and they frequently have a scrolled backboard. While some of these chests are massive affairs, given a large enough room as a setting, their excellent craftsmanship will negate their bulky size. There also are examples of chests of similar large, heavy proportions with similar drawer arrangements that do not have the overhang and probably were made between 1830 and 1870 (figure 67).

The drawers in the aforementioned chests are dovetailed, and the grain of the drawer bottoms parallels the width of the drawer. However, in many small drawers associated with these chests, the grain of the drawer bottoms often parallels the sides of the drawer. This method of construction is a likely carry-over from European craftsmanship.

The backs of some of the best made chests are of framed panels, but more commonly, the back is made of half-lapped or tongue-and-grooved vertical boards.

68. A five-drawer, pine storage chest that probably served for the storage of linen and robes. Multiple drawer, straight-front chests of this kind are not common today. Early 19th century. h: 48" x w: 32" x d: 25".

# CHAPTER TWELVE

# Washstands and Washstand-Commodes

The furniture accessories associated with personal hygiene found in the home included the washstand (*"lave-mains"*), standing quite tall on its legs, and the washstand-commode or cabinet. The latter is a case piece of furniture with a combination of at least one drawer and one door to conceal the chamber pot.

Most washstands are of light construction, with or without a hole in the top to receive the wash basin or bowl, and of rather small size, averaging about 32 inches in height. The width varies considerably from approximately 18 inches to 3 feet and the depth ranges from about 16 inches to 20 inches. Some washstands have one or more drawers immediately below the solid top (figure 70), while those with a hole in the top for the bowl are fitted with a shelf

70. This basswood washstand combines a French-Canadian folk-art splash board, a small drawer, and delicate chamfered taper legs to make a one-of-a-kind piece. Mid 19th century. h: 37½" x w: 35" x d: 20½". *From a private collection.*

69. A nicely proportioned washstand or *lave*. The scrolled backboard crested with double rolling-pin ornamentation, a single, small drawer, and the towel bars characterize many Quebec examples. Third quarter 19th century. h: 36" x w: 25½" x d: ¼". *Courtesy of Monique Shay.*

(figure 71) and sometimes a drawer close to the floor. Like other pieces of country furniture, the washstand followed along with the style of the time. Elements of the common nineteenth century styles—the Hepplewhite, Sheraton, American Empire, and the Victorian—all are to be found. The style is portrayed by the shaping of the legs, the character of the splashboard or backboard and sideboards, which together constitute the gallery, and in some cases by the towel racks, although they are not found on all washstands. Some country washstands have boldly

71. A pine and maple Empire washstand with towel bars. The curvature of the splash board and front legs are noteworthy. Mid 19th century. h: 39'' x w: 36'' x d: 21''. *Courtesy of Monique Shay.*

chamfered legs, two end stretchers, and a medial stretcher uniting the two.

The splashboard or gallery found on some country washstands is exquisitely scrolled and further adorned with cutouts, in some cases expressing a bold Québécois flavor totally independent from outside influences. It is as though some creative impulse out of the distant past had suddenly burst forth in unrestrained expression. Other splashboards, topped out with a long, turned, cylindrical roll with button or finial ends, resemble wooden rolling pins (figure 69). They are characteristically late-Empire style, quite typical of many Quebec washstands. Jean Palardy has described those stands with deeply turned legs, abundant "C" scrolls, and

ornamental curves as "Canadian Rococo".[1]

The washstand commode or cabinet was used in many homes and church related structures throughout the nineteenth century, its principle purpose the storage of the wash bowl, pitcher, chamber pot, linens, and other items related to the bath. These pieces of furniture are quite large, perhaps ranging from 2½ feet to 4 feet in width, about 18 inches to 20 inches deep, and averaging 32 inches in height. The early ones of pine or butternut consist of one or two drawers immediately beneath the top, and below, one or two doors. There is usually found at the base a scrolled or scalloped apron and plain bracket feet. Some large commodes follow the more sophisticated Empire lines by having the characteristic overhang, housing one or more drawers and supporting at the top the turned or scrolled columns that extend to the feet. Between the columns and beneath the overhang there are usually two doors with sunken panels.

The doors of the very simple country-made pieces consist of plain boards mounted on butt hinges, while the early, better-made examples commonly are fitted with raised panel doors. Later examples usually have sunken panels, and it is not unusual to see examples with moldings applied to the edges of the panel along the rails and stiles, thus highlighting the panel. In other cases, shallow moldings were applied directly to the plank ends and board doors to give the effect of paneling. Once again, the individuality seen in the scrolling and other detail given to the splashboard or gallery serves to distinguish this furniture as of probable Quebec origin, although some pieces I have seen from New Brunswick are quite similar.

During the last half of the nineteenth century, factory-made commodes, first of black walnut and later of chestnut, ash, and oak, gradually replaced the individually designed and handcrafted pieces. Furniture became available through catalogue houses, and now a century later, brand new oak and maple washstands and lyre-back commodes complete with towel bar still can be purchased right out of the catalogues.

Footnote

[1] Jean Palardy, *The Early Furniture of French Canada*, p. 284.

# CHAPTER THIRTEEN

# Country Tables and Stands

Tables are very well represented among the major pieces of Quebec, nineteenth century survival furniture, probably being second only to the chairs and the several kinds of cupboards. A great many were shipped to the United States during the 1950s and 1960s when they were plentiful. Now these tables, along with so many cupboards, have been absorbed into the American mainstream of collectible antiques to such an extent that their Canadian origin often has been lost.

Québécois country tables can be categorized, like the cupboards and chairs, according to their overall form. They include those with rectangular and square tops, round, half-round or *demi-lune* tops, and oval tops. The round-top tables often have square frames. Rectangular table frames, with or without swing legs or gate legs and with the leaves hinged to the table top, are called drop-leaf tables (figure 82). The earliest drop-leaf tables made in Quebec followed along the lines of Louis XIII or William and Mary. Those of the nineteenth century often reflect the styles of that century by the kind of turning shown by their legs. The Empire and Victorian styles are readily distinguishable, even to the beginning collector (plate 2).

Many squatty tables also exist, with their thick, deeply turned Empire legs characteristic to Quebec (figures 86 and 87). The tables were made in all sizes, beginning around the middle of the nineteenth century and for about the next thirty years. It may take some adjustment by the collector to become accustomed to them, but once accepted, one can become quite attached because of their attractive, deep, well-executed turning and their usefulness for heavy work, particularly in the kitchen.

Work tables, with either square or square taper legs, also found widespread use in country Quebec during the nineteenth century. The taper-leg tables in the Hepplewhite manner no doubt reflect the influence of New England and British craftsmen.

72. A small worktable with a festooned or scrolled apron and the usual small drawer, both quite typical of many Quebec tables. Mid 19th century. h: 26'' x w: 31'' x d: 18''. *Courtesy of Monique Shay.*

There also was a variety of drop-leaf, and gate-leg tables with square legs in use at this time.

While the legs of some country tables are plain, heavy, and straight, many were beaded on the outside corner (figure 75) or boldly chamfered all around (figure 74) to give a touch of lightness and eloquence. Those tables with beaded square legs and with chamfering only on the inside corner of each leg qualify as "country Chippendale." The distinctive, elegant chamfering seen on many Québécois tables is characteristic to the Province. I concluded after examining many taper-leg tables and stands (figure 91) that country joiners in Quebec often had become

73. A white-pine worktable or tavern table. The ends of the flat, incised, dovetailed cleats are visible on the edge of the table, left and right of the drawer. h: 27" x w: 46" x d: 34¾". *From a private collection.*

74. A worktable of ash with butternut legs. Chamfered taper legs often characterize these tables. Third quarter 19th century. h: 26½" x w: 38" x d: 30¼". *From a private collection.*

75. A small, country table in birch with second-generation white-pine top. The legs are beaded on the outside corners, suggesting Anglo-American influence. Chamfering only on the inside corners of the legs from top to bottom occasionally is seen on Quebec tables, such as this one. Early 19th century. h: 22½" x w: 28" x d: 18¼". *From a private collection.*

76. Small bedside serving table with folding frame, chamfered legs, and fenced top. Late 19th century. h: 9'' x w: 24¾'' x d: 15¼''. *From a private collection.*

accustomed to making these pieces of furniture out of heavier stock than their neighbors in the United States. Perhaps that is why so many survive.

The many miscellaneous types of country tables and stands found in Quebec include: the tripod candlestand; the scarce "X"-support, pedestal candle stands; and the common taper-leg or turned-leg stands (0, 1, and 2 drawers); folding, bedside tables; washstands or *lave-mains* (figure 70); half-round or *demi-lune* tables (figure 77) with three or four legs; sawbuck; and draw tables (figure 83). The skirt on some half-round tables is cut out to feature folk-art design, and in other cases, shaped with scalloping.

In this author's estimation, the Québécois tables which are most pleasing to the eye and that highly contribute to the development of a rich, antique decor in one's present-day home are the stretcher-base work tables, sometimes called "tavern tables" (figures 79, 80, and 81). These tables, usually wider than deep (rectangular), with a medial or "H" stretcher near the floor, average from 28 inches to 32 inches in height. Exposed tenons are the rule for the medial and lateral stretchers. The late eighteenth and early nineteenth century box stretcher tables, commonly found in New England, New York, and Pennsylvania, are seldom encountered in the nineteenth century Québécois form.

77. This *demi-lune* or half-round table of Anglo-American influence has a cherry frame and legs and butternut top. Some French-Canadian made tables of this kind have a broader apron scrolled or cut out in a folk-art design. h: 30¾'' x w: 35½'' x d: 18⅞''. *From a private collection.*

78. A small, medial, stretcher-base table of pine, with a wide lap drawer. Beading is seen on the skirt and on the outside corner of the legs, where it is combined with chamfering to ornament the legs. The draw and top are not original. First quarter 19th century or slightly earlier. h: 27'' x w: 43'' x d: 23¾''. *From a private collection.*

80. A medial, stretcher-base table in the original, old blue-green paint with a scrubbed white-pine top. Many similar Quebec tables are of heavier proportions with boldly chamfered legs. h: 24½'' x w: 46'' x d: 32½''. *From a private collection.*

79. A medial, stretcher-base table with one drop leaf. Open mortise and exposed tenon joinery is visible throughout the base. The usual flat, dovetailed, incised cleats are missing, but end cleats, butting the two sides and with the top nailed to them, perform the same function. Second quarter 19th century. h: 24'' x w: 49¼'' x d: 32¾''. *From a private collection.*

81. A large, pine, stretcher-base worktable. The overall form, multiple-board top, absence of end cleats, and a small drawer typify Quebec worktables. First half 19th century. h: 29'' x w: 65'' x d: 29''. *Courtesy of Monique Shay.*

82. This Quebec, white-pine, swing-leg, drop-leaf Hepplewhite dining table is capable of seating ten people. The taper legs are of birch. The Hepplewhite style is widely represented in Britain and America and was readily adopted in Quebec. Second quarter 19th century. h: 27½" x w: 65¾" x d: 51¾". *From a private collection.*

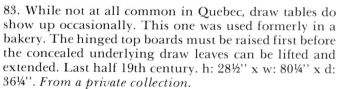

83. While not at all common in Quebec, draw tables do show up occasionally. This one was used formerly in a bakery. The hinged top boards must be raised first before the concealed underlying draw leaves can be lifted and extended. Last half 19th century. h: 28½" x w: 80¼" x d: 36¼". *From a private collection.*

84. An all yellow birch drop-leaf table in old red paint with only two end stretchers. The original, two-board top is secured with wooden pegs. Beginning of 19th century. h: 27¼" x w: 49¼" x d: 41¼". *From a private collection.*

85. The lozenge-sculptured legs of this drop-leaf table are most unusual. The joiner who made this table could have been influenced by a diamond-point *armoire.* Early 19th century. h: 27" x w: 50" x d: 47". *From a private collection.*

86. A three-board-top pine Empire table in as-found condition. The deeply turned turnip or vase-form legs reflect the return of Grecian influence. Mid 19th century. h: 27" x w: 50" x d: 36". *From a private collection.*

87. A massive dining table with Empire legs turned from 5½" stock. Third quarter 19th century. *Courtesy of Monique Shay.*

88. A 10 foot refectory table with benches, from near Baie-St.-Paul. Some tables of this form are often fitted with several drawers. Early 19th century. h: 29" x w: 122" x d: 30". *Courtesy of Pierre Constant and Orange Trading Company.*

The legs of the early nineteenth century work or tavern tables commonly are square or rectangular in cross section and either taper gently in the Hepplewhite fashion or do not taper at all. Still others are chamfered on all four corners (figure 74). Most French Canadians made the lap and/or flush drawers of these tables characteristically narrow and deep, with the drawer sides butted and nailed at the front and back. The grain of the bottom board often parallels the long direction of the drawer in the European manner.

Only some large, nineteenth-century long tables in the refectory form, descending from earlier European refectory types, retain the "H" stretcher base. The legs of many are boldly turned in the Empire or Victorian manner, while others retain either heavy chamfer or taper legs. The side and end aprons usually are fitted with several drawers (figure 88). These tables were used particularly in orphanages, nunneries, and church schools.

The tops of the wide tables generally consist of from two to five well-fitted, tongue-and-groove or plain boards secured to the frame by wooden pins. In some later examples, nails secured the tops. Flat, dovetailed, incised cleats applied to the underside of work tables served to keep the boards from curling. In New England, New York, and the Middle Atlantic States, the breadboard-style end cleat served the same purpose. Many Pennsylvania-German tables and some Ontario tables made by Pennsylvania-German immigrants have wide-board end cleats dovetailed into the underside of the tops and fitted snugly against the end skirts. A wooden peg passing through each cleat and skirt could be withdrawn to allow the top to be removed for cleaning. Rarely does one encounter such a table in Quebec, and those found there could have come from Ontario.

The use of flat, tapering, incised, dovetailed cleats is a carry-over from European joinery going back several centuries. It was and is used commonly in France, and in Dinan in Brittany, I noticed that house shutters are kept from curling by their use. The use of flat, incised cleats is not restricted totally to the French-Canadian joiner here in North America. Mennonites in several of the United States, and Hutterites and Doukhobors in Manitoba also often utilize them to keep their table tops from curling.

## Chair Tables

Chair tables, or hutch tables as they are commonly called, played an important role in furnishing some late eighteenth and nineteenth century Quebec country households too. A rather common form at the time, they have been collected so diligently that they are quite scarce today. This practical piece of furniture rests against the wall with the top up when not in use. Likewise, the top may be placed down horizontally when it is needed. The top moves on wooden pins that extend through the table's under-cleats into the chair's arms or frame. There may or may not be a drawer under the seat. Many chair tables from below the Quebec City area, particularly on the north side of the St. Lawrence, have well-turned posts (legs and their extensions) and box stretchers.

Some chair tables from the Eastern Townships have simple plain or chamfered legs and appear quite similar to northern New England forms (figure 137). Quebec-made chair tables probably represent the Anglo-American influence in Quebec.

89. The expertly turned Empire legs of this round table are its single claim to beauty. The top is a replacement. Mid 19th century. h: 28'' x diameter: 30''. *From a private collection.*

90. A small, one-drawer Quebec table or stand. The applied decorative molding at the edge of the skirt often is seen on Quebec country tables. Second quarter 19th century. h: 26¼'' x w: 26¾'' x d: 19''. *From a private collection.*

91. A small, white-pine, taper-leg, one-drawer stand from near Ayer's Cliff, Quebec. This stand clearly represents New England influence commonly seen in southern Quebec. Second quarter 19th century. h: 27'' x w: 18¾'' x d: 18½''. *From a private collection.*

92. Another lamp stand from near Richmond showing strong Anglo-American influence. Sheraton influence is seen in the thin, refined legs, turnings, and overall lightness. While stands of this kind are virtually identical on both sides of the border, there is a tendency for Canadian stands to be of larger proportions. h: 29¾'' x w: 21⅞'' x d: 17¾''. *From a private collection.*

94. A white-pine candle stand or *guéridon* with a Gothic aura about it. While its overall form suggests a late-medieval date, it could have been made as late as the early 19th century. h: 32⅛'' x w: 20½'' x d: 15''. *From a private collection.*

93. A simple country lamp stand in pine. The pedestal is crisply chamfered. Late 19th century. h: 26¾'' x w: 16'' x d: 15''. *From a private collection.*

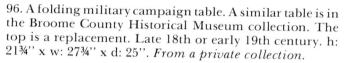

95. By any stretch of the imagination, a stand of this sort could have had several purposes, either religious, secular or both. The old red paint shows through a later coat of gray. Mid or late 19th century. h: 31'' x w: 22½'' x d: 15½''. *From a private collection.*

96. A folding military campaign table. A similar table is in the Broome County Historical Museum collection. The top is a replacement. Late 18th or early 19th century. h: 21¾'' x w: 27¾'' x d: 25''. *From a private collection.*

97. A Quebec sawbuck table with the top mortised and tenoned to the frame. A long, thick stretcher connects the two sawbuck ends. This form follows the Anglo-American tradition. Early 19th century. h: 35'' x w: 126'' x d: 29''. *Courtesy of Monique Shay.*

# CHAPTER FOURTEEN

# Chairs

98. An Ile d'Orléans birch chair with pine seat from or near the island of that name. The open mortise and tenon joinery, gentle chamfering, "H" medial stretcher base, and a rectangular framed back characterizes these chairs. The one medial back slat seen in this example often is eliminated in the initial construction. Late 18th or early 19th century. h: 32¼" x w: 14¾" x d: 12⅝" (at seat). *From a private collection.*

Many of the nineteenth century chairs seen in Quebec show strong Anglo-American influence. The exchange of information and goods between New England, New York, and Canada increased as easier transportation routes between the two countries became firmly established before the close of the first quarter of the nineteenth century. Thus, it appears that the rapidly expanding chair manufacturing industry in the United States, with its multitude of styles and varieties, soon had its effect in Canada. Canadian chair makers began to produce a great variety of half spindle-back, bow-back, step-back, arrow-back, and full-spindle Windsor chairs as well as fancy chairs similar to American Hitchcock chairs and Boston rockers. The chair makers of Quebec also developed their own innovations, resulting in some quite interesting chairs. At the same time, there was also the melding or combining of old traditional French-Canadian country styles with the new ideas from both America and Britain, resulting in a variety of attractive folk types. Hence, one might find a French-Canadian *habitant* chair showing Sheraton influence (figure 104).

The so-called primitive, country, or *habitant* chairs of the late eighteenth century continued to be made throughout the nineteenth century, including side chairs, rockers, rocking arm chairs, rocking benches, and arm chairs, as well as several kinds of children's chairs (figures 121, 122, and 124). They are of particular interest because they are distinctively French-Canadian (Québécois) with European roots. A great variety found in the Eastern Townships is indigenous to the region (figure 130).

The very similar plan of all of these chairs may be derived from country styles of continental France and possibly, to a limited extent, from Great Britain. They also share a similarity of construction and style with some Mexican chairs of the American Southwest. Basically, all of these chairs have frames in which front and back posts are rectangular or square,

99. A side view of the example in figure 98..

100. Another Ile d'Orléans chair with a box stretcher base and broad crest rail. The thick seat is shaped in this example. Early 19th century. h: 32'' x w: 16¾'' x d: 13⅞''. *From a private collection.*

101. The inspiration for shaping the backs of many French-Canadian chairs, like the one shown here on the left, no doubt came from France. The right-hand cathedral chair, reputedly from Brittany, illustrates how festooning or shaping was carried out in France. Also see figure 120. Left, h: 32¼'' x w: 15½'' x d: 13¼''; right, h: 38¾'' x w: 17¼'' x d: 14⅝''. *From a private collection.*

102. Habitant chair in maple with shaped slats. The woven seat is a recent addition. h: 35″ x w: 17¼″ x d: 15¼″. *From a private collection.*

Some chairs from the Côte de Beaupré and the Ile d'Orléans (figures 98, 99, and 100) are distinctive in that they have chamfered rectangular stretchers and seat rails instead of whittled rungs and seat rails, so common to most country or *habitant* chairs. The back consists of a plain, broad crest or top slat, below which and above the level of the seat there is occasionally one thick slat or, more commonly, no slat at all (figure 98). Some seats are of half-inch pine and are pegged to the frame; others are shaped from much thicker stock. Box or "H" stretchers strengthen the legs, the overall appearance suggesting a distant cousin to a New England country Chippendale chair. Perhaps somewhere in the remote past, they

103. A side view of the chair in figure 102 showing details of construction.

although modified by chamfering in some cases. Very often, the rungs (rounds) pass through the posts with the ends exposed (figure 102). The slats of the backs of many of these chairs penetrate or are mortised through the framing posts, thus exposing them. The chairs are handcrafted and the rungs whittled out of native hard wood—ash or birch. It seems that machine-turned stock was unknown or not available to most rural chair makers. The seats are commonly of woven material, such as splint ash, rush, or rawhide. The rockers on some of the larger chairs are very thick, with attractively scrolled upper surfaces.

have a common ancestry. These pleasing, small chairs are referred to as *Ile d'Orléans* chairs.

Another chair from the Ile d'Orleans region of special interest and not at all common anymore is the *Belle-Chasse* chair. The top slat of these chairs is very wide, commonly ranging from 6 to 8 inches, with double notching where the slat is inserted into the back posts or frame. A cutout in the form of a diamond or cross commonly adorns the center of the slat. Below the wide slat, there are usually two other, well-spaced slats, each about 1½ inches in width. A modification of this type of chair is seen in (figure 104). Other chairs with interesting cutouts come from the nearby Beaumont and St. Raphael areas east of Lévis. The country chairs of Quebec show an unending range of individuality. For example, one

105. A typical, sturdy habitant chair of ash and birch from the Montreal area. The two, closely spaced slats are characteristic of these chairs. Early to mid 19th century. h: 32¼" x w: 17¼" x d: 13½". *From a private collection.*

104. Habitant chair of possible Sheraton influence with clothespin cutouts in each slat or back rail. Beaumont area. Second quarter 19th century. h: 34" x w: 17½" x d: 14". *From a private collection.*

106. The rawhide snowshoe-weave seat on this chair is probably a replacement for the original rush seat. Rush-seat chairs were originally inventoried as *"chaise à la capucine"*. Early 19th century. h: 34¾" x w: 18" x d: 13¼". *From a private collection.*

107. A two-slat, slat-back chair in maple from the Lotbinière district. A simple chair showing great strength of character. Early 19th century. h: 35" x w: 15¾" x d: 14¾". *From a private collection.*

108. A rabbit-ear, slat-back habitant chair of delicate proportions featuring chamfered back posts and front legs. Not a common form. Probably mid-19th century. h: 36½" x w: 17" x d: 13". *From a private collection.*

*habitant* chair owned by Maurice LeMay has the rungs inserted into the legs on the diagonal so that when viewed from a distance, one sees an "X" frame supporting the lower portion of the chair (figure 111).

The backs of Québécois chairs vary greatly. Slat-back chairs usually have from 2 to 4 slats (figures 106, 107, and 108) of constant or variable widths, while splat-back chairs usually have 2, 3, 4, or more splats, depending on the width of the chair. The slats and splats are sometimes notched and adorned in folk art patterns, including cut-out hearts, diamonds, disks, stars, etc., depending on the whim or design of the maker. Chip-carved splats and slats adorn a few known examples. The range of chair construction runs from excellent to crude, with all gradations found between the extremes. The French-Canadian chair maker has found in the *habitant* chair an excellent medium in which to demonstrate his artistic expression.

109. Habitant chair combining French-Canadian elements (the frame and two slats below the crest rail) with American-inspired rabbit-ear or thumb-back rear posts (see figure 110). Second quarter 19th century. h: 33¼'' x w: 19¾'' x d: 13¾''. *From a private collection.*

111. An X-rung habitant chair of considerable ingenuity and tremendous strength. This chair could be unique. Probably last half 19th century. *Courtesy of Maurice LeMay.*

110. A Sheraton-inspired New England thumb-back or rabbit-ear plankseat chair, circa 1830. Note the similarity of the thumb-backs in this chair and the one in figure 109. h: 34½'' x w: 15'' x d: 15¾''. *Courtesy of Mark and Sally Bergland.*

112. Two, 4-half spindle, plank-seat side chairs showing strong American influence from near Montreal. On many American-made chairs, the angular corners of the crest rail are rounded. Second quarter 19th century. Left, h: 33½'' x w: 14½'' x d: 14ï''; right, h: 33'' x w: 14½'' x d: 14¾''. *From a private collection.*

114. A pair of 5-spindle Windsor chairs from the Eastern Township and very similar to many American-made chairs. The heavier spindles are characteristic of Quebec. Second quarter 19th century. h: 31⅛'' x w: 14½'' x d: 14⅞''. *From a private collection.*

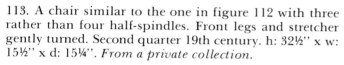

113. A chair similar to the one in figure 112 with three rather than four half-spindles. Front legs and stretcher gently turned. Second quarter 19th century. h: 32½" x w: 15½" x d: 15¼". *From a private collection.*

115. Painting entitled "End of the Line or Ripe for Restoration", by Fred E. Johansson. *Courtesy of Frederick and Lynne Johansson.*

116. A large rocking chair with mortised flat arms, from the Eastern Townships. This chair retains much of the old mustard-yellow paint. Rockers are attached to frame with bolts and nuts. Mid 19th century. h: 45" x w: 21½" x d: 16½". *From a private collection.*

117. Habitant rocking chair with two medial slats. Snow-shoe-weave seats are plentiful in Quebec. Last half 19th century. h: 35¼'' x w: 16¼'' x d: 13''. *From a private collection.*

118. The acorn finials and scrolled crest rail or top slat are two interesting refinements. Acorn finials are seldom seen on Quebec chairs. The woven backing on the chair suggests late Victorian or possibly Shaker influence. h: 39½'' x w: 17½'' x d: 14⅜''. *From a private collection.*

119. The diagonal chair rungs, also serving as braces, are quite unusual. The sweeping curve of each back post is well-executed. Mid 19th century. h: 35½'' x w: 15½'' x d: 14''. *Courtesy of Peter and Monika Johansson.*

120. The deep-set desire on the part of the maker for artistic expression is seen in the shaped slats of this *habitant* rocker. Could he have known that another maker more than three thousand miles away had the same feeling ( see figure 101)? h: 36'' x w: 19'' x d: 16''. *From a private collection.*

121. Two children's maple and ash high chairs, one with a woven seat, the other, a board seat. The left hand chair dates to mid-19th century; the other, late 19th or early 20th century. Left, h: 32¼'' x w: 12⅝'' x d: 11½''; right, h: 36¾'' x w: 14½'' x d: 13¾''. *From a private collection.*

122. A very appealing child's chair because of its proportions and fetching splay to the legs. Mid-19th century. h: 30" x w: 14" x d: 11¼". *From a private collection.*

123. A Quebec rabbit-ear or thumb-back high chair, in every respect the same as our New England chairs. Second quarter 19th century. h: 33¼" x w: 12" x d: 13¼". *From a private collection.*

124. Three children's rocking chairs. The chairs on the left and right, with the rungs doweled through the legs and tenon-and-mortise crest rails date from the 19th century. The chair in the middle of nailed construction dates from the early 20th century. Left, h: 24¾" x w: 14" x d: 11¾"; right, h: 25⅞" x w: 12¾" x d: 11½"; center, h: 23½" x w: 17" x d: 12¾". *From a private collection.*

The thin, hand-fashioned arms of arm chairs usually are fitted to slope forward (figures 125 and 127). This is seldom seen in nineteenth century chairs made in the Northern United States, with the exception of some of the chairs belonging to the Boston rocker clan. While some arms are plain and straight, others are sinuously curved in a pleasing fashion. Not infrequently, the arms are terminated by a thick, horizontally or vertically oriented, tightly coiled, snail-like hand grip (figure 126). The upper end of each back post of some high-back rocking chairs terminates in a tight, snail-like coil, too. In others, a shaped-board head rest is attached to the upper end of each back post.

Gigantic porch rockers, capable of comfortably seating a three-hundred-pound person, appeared in the late nineteenth and early twentieth century. These chairs, with heavy woven seats, and occasionally woven backs, too, were commonly turned from 6 inch stock. Both splat-back and slat-back chairs also occur, and in most cases, the flat arms are very broad. Many of these chairs were made in the Trois Rivières area.

126. Occasionally one finds a country arm rocking chair with back braces, but they are not common. Mid 19th century. h: 41'' x w: 17½'' x d: 14''. *From a private collection.*

125. A rocker from the southern Eastern Townships showing characteristic Quebec-style sloping arms. Otherwise the chair is similar to some Upstate New York and New England chairs. *Courtesy of Brain Dumoulin.*

127. A *habitant* arm rocking chair from the Eastern Townships. Mid 19th century. h: 37'' x w: 19'' x d: 16''. *From a private collection.*

128. The curvature of the back posts, sloping arms (one replaced), heavy rockers, and doweled-through rungs epitomize Québécois arm rocking chairs. Mid-19th century. *From a private collection.*

129. The heart and clothespin cutouts make for an interesting chair, perhaps a betrothal. Chairs with woven backs are not particularly common (see figure 104). Mid 19th century. Probably from the Beaumont area. h: 36" x w: 18¼" x d: 14⅞". *From a private collection.*

130. Three Eastern Township country rockers showing considerable range of form. Last half 19th century. *Courtesy of Colin MacLeod.*

131. A New England country Chippendale rocking chair. The simplicity of form seen in the frame is not far removed from that of the *habitant chair* of Quebec. Late 18th century. h: 40¼'' x w: 22¼'' x d: 15½''. *From a private collection.*

132. The arms of this sturdy rocking chair were clearly inspired by those of the American Lincoln rocker. Mid 19th century. *Courtesy of Cynthia Ballyntine.*

133. The arms and back above the seat rail show Louis XIII influence, but because of the form of the legs and doweled-through rungs, a later date is suggested. Late 18th or early 19th century. h: 39¼'' x w: 21¾'' x d: 20''. *Courtesy of Jennifer Mange, Historic Deerfield.*

134. The thick, heavy shaped arm and grip, together with chamfered supports, epitomize the early 19th century Quebec arm chair. *From a private collection.*

135. An arm chair (*fauteuil*) in as-found condition. Examination of this chair reveals that it once had a higher back with a crest rail or top slat that was tied to the medial slat by two, shaped vertical splats. Early 19th century. h: 35'' x w: 21½'' x d: 18½''. *From a private collection.*

136. An imposing *habitant* arm chair. The shaped crest, sloped arms and doweled-through rungs and seat rails characterize Quebec-made chairs. The question remains unanswered: '' ''Why should master *habitant* chairs like this one be so large and most *habitant* side chairs be so small for people of average stature?'' Early 19th century. h: 40¼'' x w: 21⅞'' x d: 18½''. *From a private collection.*

137. A white-pine chair table, or hutch table, of the form commonly seen in Southern Quebec and New Brunswick. First half of 19th century. Other examples, often with turned legs, come from the St. Lawrence River Valley, particularly below Quebec. h: 28'' x w: 44'' (top) x w: 21'' (base). *Courtesy of Hart-Smith.*

# CHAPTER FIFTEEN

# Benches and Stools

138. A three-leg kitchen stool with decked stretchers, proving maximum strength. Last half 19th century. h: 22¼'' x w: 16'' x d: 8¼''. *From a private collection.*

A variety of low benches was made in rural Quebec during the nineteenth century, many not particularly distinctive in their design or inspiration. Often they are similar to nineteenth century types made in eastern America, particularly Pennsylvania. Pickers and collectors brought large quantities to the United States because they blended beautifully with other Canadian and American pine pieces of furniture. Their length varied according to need from perhaps the width of two seated adults to ten or twelve feet. Long benches originally were used to accommodate several people seated in a row at a refectory table or a long kitchen table during meals times. At one time, hardly a porch in rural Quebec lacked a long bench.

The board legs or ends are secured to the bench top by mortise and tenon construction in the better examples, and in the poorer examples, by a housed joint and nailed. The supporting legs can be plain boards with parallel sides, or they can taper slightly outward from top to bottom. The latter is character-istic of many Québécois benches. Half-moon or boot-jack cutouts found on the board ends of some benches add a little more style. The board legs of some of the examples predating the nineteenth century are scrolled in a pleasing lyre form and in some cases, a medial stretcher has been added for extra strength. Some other nineteenth century benches are supported at each end by two sturdy, rectangular or square raked legs with framed stretchers, following a technique dating back to a much earlier time. A common practice in some areas of Quebec was to add a narrow, plain or gently scrolled skirt to the front and back sides of the bench (side pieces). In other areas, I have found them to be totally absent.

The development of a bench with a back and arms, called a settee, is a natural outgrowth from the plain, low bench. The continuous tall back posts of the settee are united at the top by a crest rail and the space between the crest rail, and the seat or rear seat rail is

139. The flat, incised, dovetailed cleat, the chamfered legs, and the strength of form portrayed by this shop stool are its highlights. Mid 19th century. h: 24½" x w: 11⅝" x d: 12¼". *From a private collection.*

either left open or filled. If the space is filled, it is usually with raised or sunken panels, splats or spindles. Vase-back splats, reflecting the late-Empire style, are quiet common. Neo-Gothic arches sometimes were cut into broad back splats, producing an interesting effect too. The better late-eighteenth and early-nineteenth century benches or settees are of solid construction with all major elements united by mortise and tenon construction and an "H" stretcher base utilized for maximum strength (145). By the mid-nineteenth century and later, many country benches or settees were made with lighter frames, often incorporating half-lap joints in place of mortise and tenon joinery (figure 144).

Many of the nineteenth century Windsor-style, plank seat, spindle-back church benches or settees found in southern Quebec are identical to New England examples, with the exception that the spindles are apt to be thicker. The back and arms tie into the plank seat, remaining separate from the understructure.

A solid end bench or settee is constructed from one board at each end with the part above the seat level shaped by an in-and-out curve or scroll. The back portion between the end boards and above the seat usually is paneled. The square or rectangular sunken panels found in many nineteenth century benches are highlighted by moldings applied to the stiles and rails of each panel.

140. A primitive white-pine bench occasionally used for resting while operating the wool wheel. Mid or late 19th century. h: 24¾" x w: 32³ᵢ" x d: 9¾". *From a private collection.*

141. These stools found in Quebec are noteworthy because of the crisp splay and chamfer shown by the legs. Last half 19th century. Left, h: 22¼" x w: 16" x d: 8¼"; right, h: 21½" x w: 17¼" x d: 10". *From a private collection.*

142. A skirted, yellow-birch low bench or stool fashioned in the Anglo-American manner. First quarter 19th century. h: 10¼" x w: 23½" x d: 9". *From a private collection.*

A form characteristic of Quebec and some of its people is the bench bed (*banc lit*) or "beggar's bed" (figures 146, 147, and 148). It appears to have been introduced early in the nineteenth century by the Irish, perhaps when newly mustered out soldiers arrived from the British Isles upon the cessation of the Napoleonic Wars. The bench bed is made so that the seat and front or facing board beneath the seat, upon unhooking, fold out to make a bed averaging about 3 feet in width. The back of a bench bed may be made of spindles (figure 146) or splats contained within the rails or it may be solid, consisting of several framed panels (see Kettle, p. 69). Plain board construction is also seen in some crude examples (figure 148). The crest rails are plain or shaped. Application of moldings and lozenges to the back board and facing board beneath the seat adds an element of style. The two enclosing ends of the bench bed are usually shaped by scrolling above the level of the seat to the crest rail. Sometimes sloping arms enclose the ends of the seat.

143. A common, Québécois white-pine kneeler or church kneeling bench. The supports of the early and middle 19th century benches are held by a mortised and tenoned joint, whereas later examples are likely to be fitted to a housed joint or rabbet and nailed. h: 7½" x w: 53¼" x d: 4¾". *From a private collection.*

144. Two, eight foot rural church benches. Mortised and tenoned stretchers unite the legs and half-lap joints unite the two back rails to the back posts. Last half 19th century. h: 31" x w: 96" x d: 14½". *Courtesy of Rodney Lloyd.*

145. A solid, pine and birch church bench of mortise-and-tenon construction throughout. The medial stretcher base is quite typical for this form. Early 19th century. h: 76'' x w: 36'' x d: 16''. *Courtesy of Monique Shay.*

146. A *banc-lit* or bench bed representative of the Irish influence in Quebec. The neatly turned Neoclassical spindles contribute a finished appearance. The seat and front or facing board fold outwardly to make a bed. Second quarter 19th century. *Courtesy of Rene Beaudoin.*

The bench chest is similar in form to the bench bed, except that it does not open up to make a bed. The seat of the bench chest is hinged to the frame, providing easy access to the storage area.

A variety of low stools (footstools or crickets) also are found in Quebec. Their construction and style is so much like the American types that frequently it is impossible to distinguish them. Yellow birch appears to have been employed most often in Canada for making footstools, but examples in pine, butternut, maple, cherry, and other wood exist, too. The solid board ends or legs were joined to the top board or seat by housed joints and nailed, or by mortise and tenon. The board ends were cut out in the form of a boot-jack or crescent and a narrow skirt usually applied to the front and back at seat level (figure 142). Some barn stools were no more than a board with three or four, short, canted broom-handle legs, each held in place by an end wedge.

147. This mid 19th-century bench bed from Quebec, and now in the Historic Deerfield collection, illustrates how mortise-and tenon construction was utilized to join the heavy frame and unite the sloping arms to the body. h: 36" x w: 74½" x d: 26". *Courtesy of Jennifer Mange, Historic Deerfield.*

The low, narrow benches, or kneelers (figure 143), so often used at church are very typical of Quebec. Many are made of pine and are at the most 6 to 8 inches high and commonly range from 2 to 6 feet in length. The two short board legs are held in place by mortise-and-tenon construction, or in later examples, by housed joints and nailed.

High stools had their place in the rural Quebec farmhouses of the nineteenth century. Those with three legs mounted into a long, narrow, thick board were used when a person rested while at the wool wheel (figure 140). Still other stools, often with boldly canted legs, served as important adjuncts in the kitchen area. A more refined, yet strong, stool that often was used in the kitchen consisted of three octagonal, canted legs mounted firmly in a thick, solid, round seat (figure 138). Close to the base, the legs were connected by decked rounds, or rungs. Heavy, four-legged stools filled a need in farm dependencies, such as the blacksmith or harness shop. A flat, incised cleat strengthened the thick seat in some of these stools (figure 139).

148. A small, plain, pine-board *banc-lit* or bench bed, with scrolled end boards. Mid 19th century. h: 33½" x w: 65" x d: 19". *Courtesy of Monique Shay.*

# CHAPTER SIXTEEN

# Beds and Cradles

Many nineteenth century bedsteads from Quebec follow along Anglo-American lines of style, basically the same as we see just to the south in the United States. The major styles of the nineteenth century are represented, including Hepplewhite, Sheraton (Federal), American Empire, Victorian, and the spool-turned style of 1850-1890. Although tall, four-post bedsteads, complete with testers or canopies, carried over into the nineteenth century, they declined in importance and gradually disappeared. Many suffered the fate of having the tall posts cut off, and by the 1830s, canopy bedsteads, for the most part, gave way to the low-post, American-Empire style.

Survival forms of country Quebec bedsteads most commonly encountered are American Empire, Victorian, and spool-and-knob turned. The Victorian and spool-and-knob turned types were widely distributed throughout the province. Canadian turners produced some handsome examples of maple

four-poster, American-Empire style rope beds with cannonball finials (figure 151) and scrolled or shaped head and footboards. Occasionally turned blanket rails replaced the scrolled footboards. Undoubtedly, some bedsteads made their way to Canada from New York and Vermont, where they were commonplace. French-Empire style sleigh beds also appeared in country Quebec during the second quarter of the nineteenth century. A great many were factory-made and identical to those seen in the United States.

Many unsophisticated, low-post, country bedsteads of no particular style, ranging from child to adult size, were individually made during the second and third quarters of the nineteenth century. The child's bed is framed on the sides and ends by two or three parallel rails or side pieces (figures 149 and 150). The lowermost side and end pieces are usually the widest, except in those with a wide headboard. The side and end pieces or rails are joined to the posts

149. A country, two-rail child's bedstead. The heavy chamfered posts and shaped headboard are characteristic. Extra large wooden pins keep the mortise-and-tenon joints snug. Simple, plain beds of this kind were made in great numbers in a land where very large families were the rule. Mid 19th century. h: 30¾'' x w: 54½'' x d: 30''. *From a private collection.*

150. Another country bed with exceptionally well-chamfered posts and a full complement of contemporary Quebec ducks and geese. Last half 19th century. *Courtesy of Brian DuMoulin.*

151. Headboard from a Quebec cannonball bed of a type commonly seen in northern New England. Second quarter 19th century. h: 42¾ x w: 51½". *From a private collection.*

by mortise-and-tenon construction and held tightly by thick wooden pins or dowels. The posts are boldly chamfered above and below the rails. An inside support rail nailed to each end of the bed received the slats.

The adult bedsteads include rope beds or cots with only a single set of heavy side and end rails to which the rope is strung. This arrangement must have presented quite a challenge for the user. Other full-size beds have matching head and footboards joined to chamfered posts of equal size. These bedsteads appear to be of British Cottage tradition and could have been introduced into Quebec by Irish and Scottish immigrants following the Napoleonic Wars. The nineteenth-century settle or bench bed (*banc lit*) is also of the Irish tradition and is discussed in the section dealing with benches.

There are also numerous late nineteenth century children's beds made of ash whose side and end boards are mortised and pinned to the four square corner posts in order to provide strength and support. The corner posts usually have turned feet and button-turned caps.

The late eighteenth and early nineteenth century pine cradles of Quebec are recognized as being remarkably distinctive because of their four long, canted posts, very heavy and often scrolled rockers, and their overall large size. They commonly range in length from 3 feet to 3½ feet. Many also have tremendous decorative appeal; therefore, great quantities were shipped to antique dealers across Canada and the United States during the 1950s and 1960s.

The simplest cradles have two end and two side boards, of which the headboard is often shaped. All four are framed by the posts into which they are tenoned and snugly pinned. Paneled cradles usually have a sunken panel at each end and two sunken panels on each side, with moldings sometimes accentuating the panels. No two cradles appear to have the posts turned identically, and this variation in itself makes an interesting study. Spool, ball, ring, baluster, vase, and various combinations are represented, with special emphasis on late-Sheraton and American-Empire style turning. Almost always terminating in a button or knob, the posts are attached to the rockers by means of a half-lap joint and pinned. Some rockers are about three inches thick and certainly look as though they were made to last forever. The posts and rockers are commonly of birch. The square posts of a few cradles are attractively chamfered and topped with a button or knob.

Anglo-American style, open and hooded pine cradles of more delicate proportions also were fashioned in Quebec. Cradles of this kind from the southern Eastern Townships show strong affinity to those of neighboring Vermont.

During the Victorian era, numerous factory-made spindle cradles and cribs were made available to the rural populous. These usually consisted of closely spaced spool or similarly turned spindles framed on all four sides by the upper and lower rails. The four corner posts, often turned, received the rails. The head end of the crib or cradle usually was modified by a gabled pediment enclosing small, variously turned spindles. If rockers were applied to the foot end of the posts, it became a cradle; otherwise, it was a small crib.

152. A cradle in white pine with turned maple posts and birch rockers. Many Quebec cradles have longer posts and thicker rockers than in this example. First quarter 19th century. h: 29'' x w: 37'' x d: 31'' (at rockers). *From a private collection.*

153. The extended posts, frame construction, and thick, half-moon rockers characterize this cradle from the lower St. Lawrence region. Late 18th or early 19th century. h: 23¼'' x w: 37¾'' x d: 28½'' (at rockers). *Courtesy of Jennifer Mange, Historic Deerfield.*

# CHAPTER SEVENTEEN

# Desks

Country-made desks of pine and butternut and formal fall-front and kneehole desks of exotic and native hardwoods appeared in Quebec during the late eighteenth and early nineteenth centuries. Late nineteenth century country desks often were made of ash. The formal mahogany desks, used by business, government, and church officials, were probably unaffordable for the average *habitant*.

In general, two types of country-style desks were extensively utilized during the nineteenth century in rural Quebec. They were the desks standing on legs and those without legs made to rest on the surface of a table or stand. The four legs of the standing desks were mortised to receive the tenons of the front, back, and two side boards making up the body of the desk. The inclined writing surface was hinged to a flat-top board near the back of the desk top. A scrolled or notched gallery, having a distinct Québécois flavor, may have been added. The bottom of the desk was snugly fitted to the sides and held fast by wooden pegs or nails. Desks of this kind stand about 30 to 36 inches above the floor on square, square-tapered (figure 154), or appropriately turned legs (figure 156). These old desks, many of which were used in schools, have found new uses today in the kitchen and also as telephone stands.

Other desks similarly constructed but perhaps 6 to 8 feet in width were made to accommodate several students seated next to each other on a bench. The student could store belongings on a shelf constructed a few inches below the fixed, sloping top.

A desk without legs was, in reality, a rectangular box with a slanted or inclined writing surface, usually butt-hinged to a horizontal top board. In some cases, one or more drawers are found below the inclined writing surface. Examples also exist with the space below the writing surface left open so that the bottom of the desk served as a storage shelf. An integral part of some country desks was a nest of pigeonholes, with or without doors, rising at the back of the desk (figure 155).

154. A small school desk of white-pine with oak legs. Many similar desks from Quebec have taper or turned legs. Third quarter 19th century. h: 34½" x w: 25¼" x d: 20¾". *From a private collection.*

Some desk boxes are fitted into a rectangular frame on legs which may or may not have stretchers near the base. Typically an Anglo-American form, a desk of this type is called a desk-on-frame. Tavern keepers, school-masters, and merchants made widespread use of these desks in Vermont and New Hampshire. In all probability, northern New Englanders who settled in southern Quebec continued to make them well into the nineteenth century. Examples found in the Eastern Townships, with late-Sheraton style turned legs, could represent the influence of British immigrants who arrived after 1815.

155. A white-pine table desk used for mail. At one time, it had more pigeonholes. A barely visible ink stamp impression on the slanted surface says "Paid". Mid 19th century. h: 21½" x w: 32¼" x d: 25⅛". *From a private collection.*

156. A small, lift-top, turned-leg, white-pine school desk in as-found condition. Mid 19th century. h: 28" x w: 20¾" x d: 20". *Courtesy of Georges Porier.*

# CHAPTER EIGHTEEN

# Flax and Wool Wheels

The large, Quebec spinning wheel was, without doubt, the single piece of Canadian "furniture" that made the greatest impression on the antique-hungry American buying public. During the 1950s and 1960s, every antique-minded, aspiring young homemaker had to have one. As a result of this strong demand, truckload after truckload of Canadian spinning wheels made their way through New England and New York to distant points across the United States. At the same time, demand grew for the wheels in Ontario and other Provinces to the west in Canada. One dealer in Greenfield, Massachusetts, told me that he had handled "hundreds of them." Now, some twenty years later, these wheels have become difficult to find and so scattered that their true provenance, in many cases, has been lost.

The large wheels to which I am referring (figures 157 and 159) were attractive, commonplace forms found throughout French-speaking Quebec. Various combinations of birch, ash, and maple were used in their construction. Turners in small shops put earlier models together, while later models, made as late as the early twentieth century, were mass produced. Many of the factory-made examples from St. Hyacynth and Kamouraska have a cast iron foot pedal, while earlier examples usually have wooden pedals. In either case, pressing the pedal activates the wheel. The wheels of these highly efficient machines are about 30 inches in diameter, a full one-third larger than the Saxony or Brunswick wheel (figure 158), which is about 18 to 20 inches in diameter. The latter was used extensively in New England during the late eighteenth century and early nineteenth century, and ever since then has been called a flax wheel, and it's known by some as a "Spinning Jenny."

While the "age of homespun" appears to have continued into the twentieth century in some secular and religious quarters in Quebec, thousands of French-Canadians left their farm homes to put their

157. Large-wheel Quebec flax wheel with turned spokes and cast iron foot pedal. Brought to Athol (MA) from Quebec by the Brouillet family in 1887. Fourth quarter 19th century. *Courtesy of the Athol (Massachusetts) Historical Society.*

skill to work in newly developing textile factories in Canada, the New England states, and New York state during the late nineteenth century and early twentieth century. Spinners in Quebec and other parts of Canada and the United States made wide use of the ubiquitous wool wheel, too. This, the largest of the spinning wheels, commonly has a wheel diameter of about 42 inches. The wool wheel is operated by hand or a wheel finger, in reality a shaped stick of wood 6 to 8 inches or more in length. Other smaller wheels of Continental design were used in Quebec from the early settlement days, but they cannot be considered original designs in the province. It is the extra large size spinning wheel that may merit that honor.

158. A New England flax, Saxony or Brunswick wheel. This type of wheel is about one-third smaller than the conventional Quebec flax wheel. Late 18th or early 19th century. *Courtesy of the Athol (Massachusetts) Historical Society.*

159. Another large-wheel flax wheel. Wheels of this type were shipped to the States in the 1950s by the thousands . Fourth quarter 19th century. h: 43½'' x w: 27'' (at table) x d: 21½'' (at base). *Courtesy of Fred and Sue Hellen.*

# CHAPTER NINETEEN

# Yarn Winders or Reels

The yarn winder or reel was found on the habitant's porch in summer and in the warm kitchen in winter, always accompanying the spinning wheel. Examination of the Quebec yarn winder shows that this popular, simple machine consists of two parts: the moving part (called the reel) and the stationary supporting frame. The frame stands on shoe feet, in many examples. The yarn was wound around the four bars that make up the reel. Each bar is supported by a pair of arms radiating from the axle, which is seated in the two upright supports of the frame. A wooden crank extending from one end of the axle operates the reel. A majority of these well-made winders exhibit mortise-and-tenon construction, with the tenons usually exposed. This form (figure 163), like the large flax spinning wheel, was widely dispersed across Canada and the United States in the 1950s and 1960s by antique dealers and collectors. The yarn winders of Quebec differ appreciably in form and are generally less refined than the Anglo-American clock-and-click reel winder.

160. A beautifully crafted, four-spoke yarn wheel from the Eastern Townships. Second or third quarter 19th century. h: 39¼'' x w: 23¼'' x d: 21½''. *From a private collection.*

161. Two, handcrafted shuttles. The left hand example shows chip-carved detail. Left, h: 1'' x w: 10¼'' x d: 2⅛''; right, h: 5/16'' x w: 8'' x d: 1⅝''. *From a private collection.*

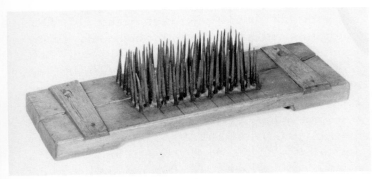

162. A Québécois hetchel showing the use of two, flat, incised dovetailed cleats. h: 5¾'' x w: 20'' x d: 7½''

164. The chamfered center post and arm supports make this a beautiful swift. Mid 19th century. h: 24'' x w: 24⅝'' x d: 24⅝''. *From a private collection.*

163. A 19th century Quebec yarn winder or reel. While once extremely common in Quebec, their numbers now are depleting rapidly. h: 24'' x w: 16¼'' x d: 20¾''. *From a private collection.*

# CHAPTER TWENTY

# Churns and Dough Boxes

During the 1950s and 1960s, antique pickers collected large churns and dough boxes by the thousands. Like the spinning wheels and yarn winders, many were transported to other parts of Canada or to the United States. Thus, examples in good condition are becoming very scarce in Quebec. In 1960, the Elliotts generally carried more than fifty churns in stock at one time.

The churn is actually a large tub contained between two pine plank ends standing on the floor (figures 169 and 170) or supported by four rectangular legs. A handled lid on the top provides access. A four-bladed paddle inside the tub is operated from the outside by a crank and shaft. The plank ends of the churn may be shaped at the base by a boot-jack, double-scroll, or crescent cutout. The rectangular legs, used for support, are arranged vertically or in sawbuck fashion and nailed or screwed to the outside of the tub.

The typical large, Québécois white pine dough box, or tray, stands on legs and is commonly 3 to 4 feet wide and about 2½ feet high (figure 165). One might suppose that the larger the box, the larger the production or the family. Regardless of their bulkiness, they were an indispensable furnishing on every Quebec farm during the nineteenth century. Each side of the dough box usually consists of one or two solid boards. The side, end, and bottom boards most commonly are butted and nailed but may be dovetailed with the bottom butted and nailed. A heavy, decorative molding often was applied to the outside near the tray bottom. All are made to receive a top or lid. The two end boards, continuous from top to bottom, serve as legs. The portion below the level of the tray bottom commonly is shaped in boot-jack fashion or scrolled in the Empire manner. In other examples, a rectangular frame, strengthened with box stretchers or an "H" stretcher, received the box.

165. A large, pine dough box or tray on legs. Dough boxes were indispensable on every farm in 19th-century Quebec. h: 31" x w: 39¼" x d: 19". *From a private collection.*

166. An Empire-style dough box in pine. This form was probably used in the Montreal district. Mid 19th century. h: 30¼″ x w: 43½″ x d: 14¾″. *Courtesy of Peter and Monika Johansson.*

167. Some dough trays were made with the plank ends extended and shaped as legs. Still others were of frame construction like this one with the extended posts serving as legs. *Courtesy of Cynthia Ballyntine.*

168. A rectilinear dough tray on legs with cleated top, possibly from the Richelieu River Valley. h: 29'' x w: 44'' x d: 22''. *Courtesy of Monique Shay.*

170. The butter churn or food mixer, like the dough tray, was a part of every farm in 19th-century Quebec. h: 31½'' x w: 18'' x d: 15⅛''. *From a private collection.*

169. A large butter churn or food mixer. Cutouts at the base are a typical Quebec form. Probably third quarter 19th century. h: 28½'' x w: 16¼'' x d: 18¼''. *Courtesy of Frederick and Lynne Johansson.*

Occasionally, one can find more elaborate dough boxes, some with framed, sunken panels on all four sides fitted to square or square-tapered legs. The raised-panel dough boxes are considered to be rare. Today, refinished dough boxes and churns on legs commonly are used as storage boxes for such diverse items as magazines, sewing and knitting material, books, or liquor.

# CHAPTER TWENTY-ONE

# Woodenware and Other Small Household Accessories

171. A primitive pine bucket bench, "right off the farm." Late 19th century. *Courtesy of Rodney Lloyd.*

An abundance of small, hand-fashioned, wooden objects were used in and about the Quebec farm kitchen during the nineteenth century. In terms of tradition and function, many resemble earlier French-Canadian, Anglo-American, and Continental forms, whose unchanged use and style extends back two centuries or more.

However, a few forms are sufficiently distinctive to label them as originating in Quebec. These include table or shelf boxes and wall boxes, made from eastern white pine or butternut, and profoundly carved, featuring the native fauna and flora, such as the beaver and the balsam fir. A few examples represent the hand of a master carver. A variety of small table boxes made out of the same kind of wood and adorned with applied lozenges and other geometrical forms or relief carving also are associated with Quebec craftsmanship (figure 16). Likewise, many of the round and oval boxes exhibiting chip carving and other ornamentation are of or may derive from the Indian heritage in Canada. The better-made square and rectangular boxes with either flat or domed hinged lids have dovetailed corners or exhibit a shouldered joint at each corner. It is interesting to note that the thin topping boards found on the small, gently domed, Quebec-made trunks often have a slight overlap, amounting to about ½" on all four sides (figure 11).

Ordinary boxes are butted at the joints, nailed, and often fitted with sliding lids. The majority are painted in subdued colors, most commonly in green, blue, brown, rust, and black. Some storage boxes have molded lids or covers that lap snugly to the box (figure 180). Many boxes also have a base molding across the front and along the sides, adding a feeling of balance and completion (figure 14). Wall boxes commonly found around the home included those used for tobacco pipes, salt storage, cutlery, and combs (figures 174, 175, 176, 177, and 200).

172. A typical, white-pine Quebec bucket or pail bench. Last half 19th century. h: 43½'' x w: 39'' x d: 13''. *Courtesy of James Prew.*

173. A country bread maker's tray and implements. 19th century. h: 3½'' x w: 34¼'' x d: 23¾''. *From a private collection.*

175. A common form of wall box found both in Quebec and the States. Slight relief was produced by shallow, straight-line gouging. Late 19th century. h: 9'' x w: 8⅜'' x d: 4½''. *From a private collection.*

174. Left to right, a lidded salt box in ash, late 19th century, and an open salt box in pine, mid 19th century. Salt boxes were hung by the kitchen stove. Left, h: 14⅝'' x w: 8¾'' x d: 7¼'' ; right, h: 15¼'' x w: 10½'' x d: 7¼''. *From a private collection.*

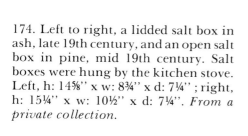

176. The form shown by this wall box, possibly used for knives, is in no way restricted to Quebec, for similar examples occur in several of the Eastern States and Ontario. First half 19th century. h: 20½'' x w: 8⅜'' x d: 4¼''. *From a private collection.*

177. An unusual wall box with four trays, possibly used for candles. The notching at the top is of particular interest, suggesting an 18th- or early 19th-century origin. h: 31⅝'' x w: 11⅞'' x d: 4⅞''. *From a private collection.*

178. An unusual, small, triangular box in old green paint. Second quarter 19th century. h: 8⅛'' x w: 15⅞'' x d: 3''. *From a private collection.*

179. This little Gothic collection box has two slots for small coins. It was probably hung in a church long ago. Last quarter 19th century. h: 10'' x w: 5⅝'' x d: 5½''. *From a private collection.*

180. The molded lids of these two painted candle boxes fit snugly. Early 19th century. Left, h: 6'' x w: 11⅛'' x d: 6¾''; right, h: 6'' x w: 12⅝'' x d: 9¾''. *From a private collection.*

181. A rare, beautifully chip-carved frame made to hold a picture or relic (*relique-contenant*) of a saint or martyr. All parts, cut from one piece of maple, are connected, hinged and were never separated. The carving includes a chip carved band or border, four lozenges, and a wheel. 18th or early 19th century. h: 13½'' x w: 4'' x d: ¾''. *From a private collection.*

182. Possibly a lace winder. The incised carving is meticulously done on this white-pine piece found in the Eastern Townships. Probably 19th century. h: 12'' x w: 4½'' x d: ½''. *From a private collection.*

183. Tobacco was an important staple in rural early Quebec. To prepare a plug of tobacco for pipe smoking, a tobacco cutter, similar to this one, was usually employed. h: 13⅛" x w: 7½" x d: 6⅛". *From a private collection.*

184. This tobacco cutter normally hung on the wall when not in use. Late 19th century. h: 18⅛" x w: 6¾" x d: ¾". *From a private collection.*

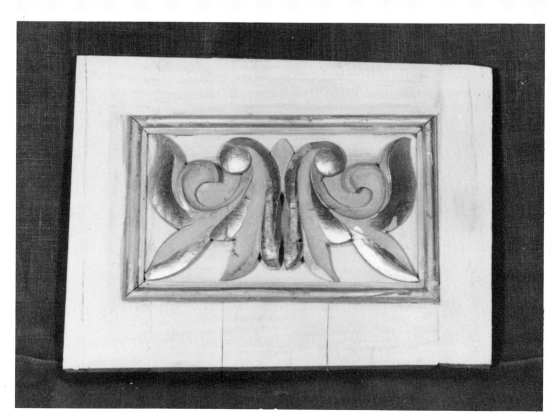

185. The nineteenth-century Quebec wood-carver's skill often was expressed in ornamental church carvings. *From a private collection.*

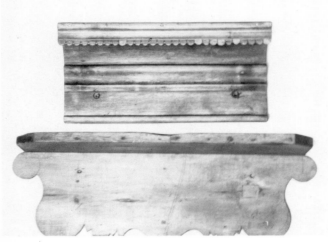

186. Two Quebec wall shelves in butternut. Festooning as seen in the upper example and scrolling in the lower were widely used in Quebec during the 19th century. Top, h: 8" x w: 18" x d: 6"; bottom, h: 9¾" x w: 30¾" x d: 7⅝". *From a private collection.*

187. This small, sophisticated bracket shelf in maple supports a Portneuf plate. Mid-19th century. *Courtesy of Cynthia Ballyntine.*

Also common in farm homes were the butter stamps featuring carved beavers, maple and palm leaves. Still other items were wooden bowls, rolling pins, cutting and kneading boards, and paddles associated with the baking of bread and rolls. Wooden maple sugar molds with such Québécois motifs as roosters, beavers, the Sacred Heart, crosses, and personal initials (figures 190, 191, 192, and 193) also enjoyed widespread use. Long, shallow troughs, closed at each end and with adjustable dividers, were commonly used in maple sugar production in Quebec during the latter part of the nineteenth century (figure 189).

A variety of small, plain and ornamental shelves or brackets served as furnishings in the country farm homes too. These consist of a graduated series of upwardly and outwardly extended moldings from bottom to top, attached to a backing board and capped with a horizontal shelf board. The moldings below the shelf are either plain or, in the case of the better examples, turned, and the backing board adorned with dentils, rosettes, carved figures, or chip carving. The simplest shelves consist of a plain or shaped horizontal board supported by one or more vertical wooden brackets nailed or screwed to the wall (figures 186, 187, and 188). These shelves supported such stationary objects as shelf clocks, crucifixes, ornamental wood carvings, lamps, and pewter and ceramic dishes. Hanging shelves with plain or scrolled end boards, designed to be easily hung up or taken down, were used for cooling and temporarily storing freshly baked goods and other food stuffs.

The bucket or pail bench (figures 171 and 172), also a common accessory, found extensive use across the province during the nineteenth century. Their contemporary appeal for displaying crockery, copperware, plants, and other objects has resulted in their present scarcity. These pine benches usually consist of two, variously spaced shelves supported by two vertical end boards. The fronts of the end boards most commonly are gently and attractively shaped above the second shelf, and often at the base, boot-jack or crescent-shaped cutouts are present. The backs of the benches are either open or boarded. In some examples, a folk art-scrolled deck surrounds the top shelf. Québécois bucket benches often are fitted with plain-board or sunken-panel doors below the first open shelf. The heavy French-Canadian examples are apt to be taller than wide, averaging about 3½ feet in height. Some of the plain benches that I have examined are virtually identical in form to those made in Eastern Pennsylvania and New Jersey.

188. The long, pine wall shelf was an indispensable item in the parlor of many Canadian farm houses. This one supports a collection of Portneuf pottery. Probably second quarter 19th century. *Courtesy of Cynthia Ballyntine.*

189. An ash sugar mold of five compartments. Last quarter 19th century. h: 25¼" x w: 6⅛" x d: 4". *From a private collection.*

190. An "initial" sugar mold carved from butternut. Late 19th century. h: 2" x w: 8¼" x d: 11¾". *From a private collection.*

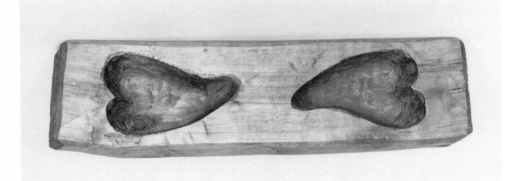

191. A French-Canadian heart sugar mold typical of the Bois Franc region. Fourth quarter 19th century. h: 16'' x w: 4¼'' x d: 2¼''. *From a private collection.*

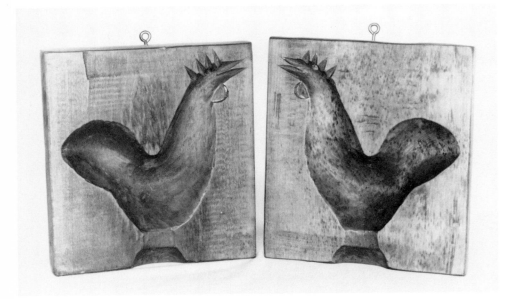

192. While only about 30 years old, this maple sugar mold is an excellent facsimile of one from the 19th century. h: 9¾'' x w: 8¾'' x d: 2¾''. *From a private collection.*

193. A scarce sugar mold in the form of a Bible. Lozenges repeat on both covers and the spine. h: 6⅛'' x w: 2'' x d: 4½''. *From a private collection.*

194. This diverse collection of woodenware includes paddles, a shuttle, butter mold, and a carved wooden hatchet case. The paddle is 24" long. *From a private collection.*

195. A small, hardwood mortar and pestle. Surprisingly few have survived. First half 19th century. h: 5½" x w: 4⅝" x d: 4⅝". *From a private collection.*

Drying racks were an indispensable part of the household furnishings too. The upright types folded and opened like a book and stood on legs (figure 198). Others consisted of two vertical arms mounted on horizontal shoe feet. Two or three, equally spaced, mortised-and-tenoned crossbars, used for airing heavy blankets, connected the arms (figure 199). A beveled or plain wooden roller, mounted between two wooden wall brackets, also served to dry towels and clothing (figure 201).

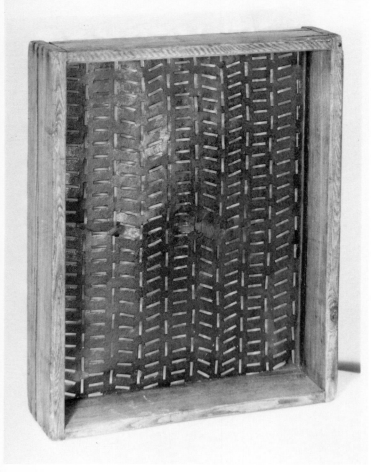

196. While this punched-tin apple drying box is from Quebec, it is virtually identical to some Pennsylvania examples. 19th century. h: 24¼" x w: 18¾" x d: 5⅜". *From a private collection.*

197. These three different knob-and-peg hangers or racks typify forms used throughout rural Quebec. 19th century. Top, h: 54" x w: 2¾" x d: 1"; middle, h: 40¾" x w: 2¾" x d: 1"; bottom, h: 37½" x w: 1½" x d: 1". *From a private collection.*

198. Folding clothes-drying rack in birch. Beading and chamfering enhance its appearance. Late 19th century. h: 32" x w: 18 15/16" x d: ⅞". *From a private collection.*

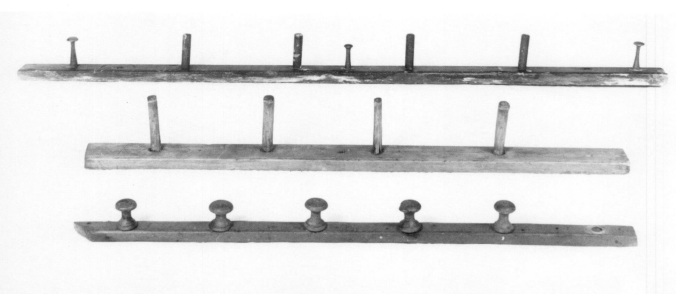

During the nineteenth century, some members of the household made interesting pine picture frames for secular and religious subjects. The frames usually were joined at each corner by either a miter joint or a half-lap joint. The surfaces of the frame might be plain and flat, molded, molded and pierced, or ornately relief-carved, which is the scarcest form. Other delightful examples are those made with cutouts depicting birds, animals, flowers, and hearts.

Handcrafted children's play furniture in the form of tables, chests of drawers or commodes, chairs, cradles, beds, armoires, and other forms was an important part of the furnishings of the *habitant* home (figures 206, 207, 208, 209, 210, and 211). These sturdy pieces, usually of the same material and fashioned in the same way as the full-sized examples, are scarce today.

Enrichment of small wooden household accessories seen around the home often was accomplished by chip-carving. More than one *habitant* was very

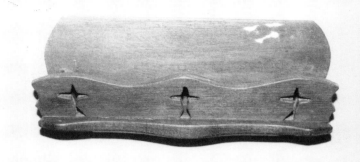

200. A comb box with cutouts in the Québécois manner, fashioned from mahogany. Late 19th or early 20th century. h: 21¼'' x w: 11¼'' x d: 2¼''. *From a private collection.*

201. From the wear seen on the brackets, this pine and maple towel rack served much time. Mid 19th century. h: 10⅞'' x w: 17⅞'' x d: 3½'' (including backing). *From a private collection.*

199. A mortised and tenoned drying rack with shoe feet in the Anglo-American tradition from Ulverton, Quebec. Early 19th century. h: 50½'' x w: 26¼'' x d: 12''. *From a private collection.*

skillful at this form of low-relief carving (figures 181 and 182). High-relief carving has been performed in Quebec by skilled artisans for more than three centuries and continues to be practiced today, especially in the St. Jean Port-Joli area. However, some of the great masterpieces were sculptured by church carvers during the eighteenth and nineteenth centuries (figure 205). Fragments and even whole pieces dispossessed by former owners occasionally are available at antique marketplaces.

## GAME BOARDS AND CHILDREN'S ACCESSORIES

Many country families played chess, checkers, Parcheesi, and other games to help pass the long, cold Quebec winters. They used a variety of game boards, mostly of home manufacture (figures 202, 203, and 204). There were small boards for children, and others so large that they fully occupied the top of a small, round table, at which several people could be seated. Twelve-grid, twelve-by-nine, ten-grid, and eight-grid examples, as well as other grid combinations, are seen occasionally. The more grids on a board, the longer it would take to play a game, which was no hardship during the long evenings.

The original molding or fence on the better boards is well-executed and held by square nails, but occasionally some or all of the molding has been replaced because of rough usage. The squares are commonly painted, and in a few cases are handsomely carved (figure 204). Some boards still retain the ring with which the board was hung on a wall when not in use (figure 202).

The best boards display the original paint. The trays at each end of the board may be painted with geometric designs or, rarely, with a scene depicting the owner's or forebear's home. Others are carefully initialed. The original quality of the lines, initialing, painting, and color harmony determine the value of the boards. They have an appealing sense of compatibility displayed with country pine and butternut furniture.

202. An early pine game board of 9 x 12 squares with original hanger. Who was A.M.? 19th century. h: 28'' x w: 16½'' x d: 15/16''. *From a private collection.*

203. A butternut game board with 12 x 12 squares. Late 19th century. *From a private collection.*

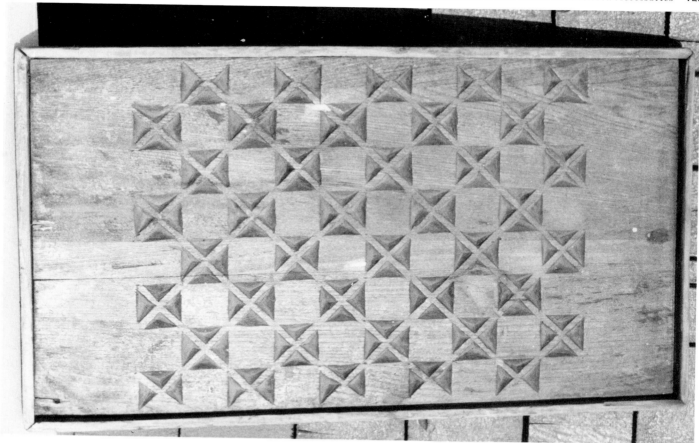

204. This carved game board of 8 x 10 squares is in butternut. There is no tray at either end. Late 19th or early 20th century. *Courtesy of Jean Deshaies.*

205. This excellent painted pine carving of a bird, vine, and foliage was found in the storage area of a church in central-southern Quebec. Many church carvers were at work during the 19th century. *Courtesy of Guy Boucher.*

206. A well-proportioned child's doll table with a similarly molded top and skirt. The turned legs are of interest. Last third 19th century. h: 16⅞" x w: 21" x d: 15⅜". *From a private collection.*

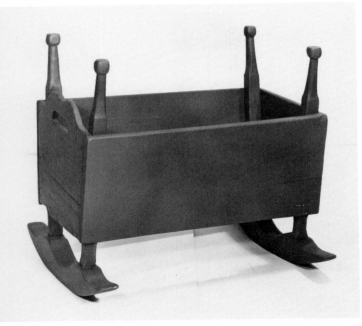

207. This handcrafted doll's cradle no doubt saw service for a long time during and after the 19th century. The shaping of the long corner posts is characteristic of Quebec. One rocker replaced. h: 17¾'' x w: 18⅜'' x d: 16⅝''. *From a private collection.*

209. A scarce, finely proportioned child's toy *armoire* in white pine with original paint. Early 19th century. h: 22⅛'' x w: 19¾'' x d: 12½''. *From a private collection.*

208. This handsome, *petite armoire* illustrates the use of post-and-frame construction in small pieces of furniture. The inset panels, applied moldings, and flush doors mounted on butt hinges suggest an early 19th century date. h: 23⅜'' x w: 19½'' x d: 11½''. *Courtesy of Jennifer Mange, Historic Deerfield.*

210. A plain-board-door, child's toy *armoire*. Mid 19th century. h: 24⅜'' x w: 14'' x d: 10½''. *From a private collection.*

211. A child's Empire-style bonnet chest in white pine. Regardless of the size, bonnet chests usually have in their superstructure two large drawers, one to the left and one to the right flanking two or more small medial drawers. Mid 19th century. *Courtesy of Cynthia Ballyntine.*

## WOODEN CANDLESTICKS, TORCHERES AND FIREPLACE ACCESSORIES

We were impressed with the great variety of beautifully turned, tall, wooden candlesticks available to the collector in the 1950s and 1960s (figures 77 and 212). One could gain a feeling of style and period by carefully scrutinizing the turnings, which sometimes were covered with many years' accumulation of aluminum and other colored paints. The sticks, originally given an undercoating of red and then painted sparkling white, adorned churches and chapels across the Province. The early examples were usually turned from one piece of stock, perhaps 6 inches in diameter. The shafts of the middle and late nineteenth and early twentieth century examples usually were fitted to a separately turned base. Sometimes a wooden screw united them. Wooden ecclesiastical candlesticks were not commonly used in early New England, where brass, pewter and silver were in favor.

Wooden standards, or *torchères*, supported candlesticks and other lighting devices and continued to be made into the early twentieth century. The standard consisted of a round or rectangular cap mounted at the top of a long, neatly chamfered or turned shaft of white pine. The base of the shafts of some eighteenth and early nineteenth century examples were set into two, half-lapped crossed pieces of pine, which provided the needed balance. A few, undoubtedly, had a broad, turned base. The standards commonly ranged in height from 3 to 5 feet or more.

212. This handcrafted pine picture frame may represent the maker's rendition of the ubiquitous Victorian criss-cross walnut frame. Late 19th century. Wooden candlesticks like these were used extensively in churches and chapels. Early 19th century. Frame, h: 18" x w: 14¾" x d: 11/16"; left candlestick, h: 12¼" x w: 5¾" (at base); right candlestick, h: 14⅝" x w: 4⅜" (at base). *From a private collection.*

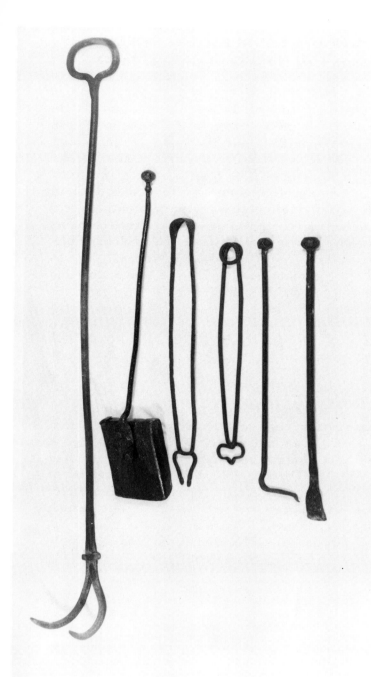

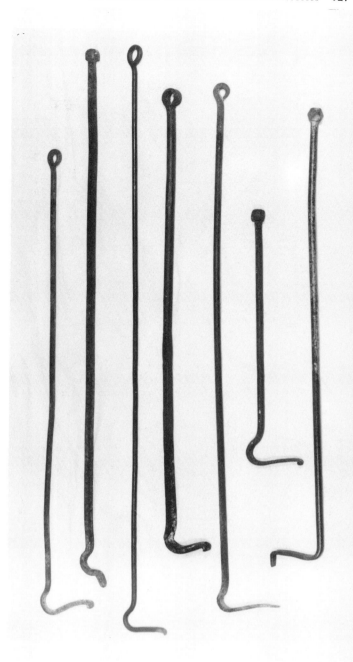

213. A grouping of 19th century wrought-iron fireplace tools. Ember tongs in center similar to forms found in Ireland. Longest utensil: 51". *From a private collection.*

214. Wrought-iron pokers of diverse forms and sizes illustrating faceted knob and loop handles and serpent-head tips. Late 18th and early 19th century. Longest poker: 44⅜".

# Bibliography

## Books & Pamphlets

Aronson, Joseph. *The Encyclopedia of Furniture*, 3rd. ed. New York: Crown Publishers, Inc., 1965.

Atto, Kathleen H. *Lennoxville (A History of Lennoxville -A Compilation, by Lennoxville-Ascot Historical and Museum Society)*. Sherbrooke: Progressive Publications, 1975.

Barbeau, Marius. *Quebec Where Ancient France Lingers*. Toronto: The MacMillan Company of Canada, 1936.

Brault, Gerard J. *The French-Canadian Heritage in New England*. Hanover (NH): University Press of New England, 1986

Channing, Marion L. *The Textile Tools of Colonial Homes*. Marion, MA: The Channings, 1969.

Cuisenier, Jean. *French Folk Art*. Tokyo, New York: Kodansha International, Ltd., 1976.

Day, C.M. *History of the Eastern Townships*. Montreal: John Lovell, Publisher., 1869.

Dobson, Henry, and Barbara Dobson. *The Early Furniture of Ontario and the Atlantic Provinces*. Toronto: M. F. Feheley Publishers Co., Ltd, 1974.

Fales, Dean A., Jr. *The Furniture of Historic Deerfield*. New York: E. P. Dutton and Co., 1976.

Finlay, A. Gregg, ed. *Heritage Furniture (of New Brunswick Museum)*. St. John: New Brunswick Museum, 1976.

Foss, Charles H. *Cabinet Makers of the Eastern Seaboard (Canada)*. Toronto: M. F. Feheley Publishers, Ltd., 1977.

Griffin, William, and Florence Griffin, et al. *Neat Pieces: The Plain Style Furniture of 19th Century Georgia*. Atlanta: W. R. C. Smith Publishing Company, 1983. (The Atlanta Historical Society)

Kalm, Peter. *The America of 1750; Peter Kalm's Travels in North America*. New York: Dover Publications, 1966.

Kelley, J. Frederick. *The Early Domestic Architecture of Connecticut*. New Haven: Yale University Press, 1927.

Kettell, Russell Hawes. *The Pine Furniture of Early New England*. New York: Dover Publications, Inc., 1956.

Kovel, Ralph, and Terry Kovel. *American Country Furniture, 1780-1875*. New York: Crown Publishers, 1965.

Lawrence, John. *The History of Stanstead County, Province of Quebec*. Montreal: Lovell Printing and Publishing Company, 1874.

Lessard, Michel, and Huguette Marquis. *Encyclopédie Des Antiquités Du Québec*. Montreal: Les Editions De L'Homme Ltee, 1971.

Lessard, Michel, and Gilles Vilandre'. *La Maison Traditionnelle Au Québec*. Montreal: Les Editions De L'Homme Ltee, 1974.

MacLaren, George E. W. *Antique Furniture by Nova Scotia Craftsmen*. Toronto: Ryerson Ltd, 1961.

Miller, Edgar G., Jr. *American Antique Furniture Vols. 1 & 2*. New York: Dover Publications, 1966.

Nutting, Wallace. *Furniture of the Pilgrim Century*. Framingham, MA: Old America Company, 1924.

Nutting, Wallace. *Furniture Treasury*. New York: The Macmillan Company, 1961.

Oglesbay, Catharine. *French Provincial Decorative Art*. New York: Bonanza Books (Crown Publishing, Inc.), 1951.

Pain, Howard. *The Heritage of Upper Canadian Furniture*. Toronto: Van Nostrand Reinhold, Ltd., 1978.

Palardy, Jean. *The Early Furniture of French Canada*. New York: St. Martins Press, 1965.

Parkman, Francis. *The Old Regime in Canada*. Boston: Little, Brown and Company, 1874.

Ryder, Huia G. *Antique Furniture by New Brunswick Craftsmen*. Toronto: McGraw-Hill Ryerson Ltd., 1966.

Shackleton, Philip. *The Furniture of Old Ontario*. Toronto: The Macmillan Company of Canada, 1973.

Shea, John G. *Antique Country Furniture of North America*. New York: Van Nostrand Reinhold Co., 1975.

Sonn, Albert H. *Early American Wrought Iron*. New York: Bonanza Books (Crown Publishers, Inc.), 1979.

Stevens, Gerald. *In A Canadian Attic*. Toronto: McGraw-Hill Ryerson Ltd., 1963.

Webster, Donald Blake. *English Canadian Furniture of the Georgian Period*. Toronto: McGraw-Hill Ryerson, Ltd., 1979.

## Periodicals

Barbeau, Marius. "Laurentian Wood Carvers." *The Magazine Antiques*, July 1934, pp. 14-16.

Chevalier, M. Jean Guy, ed. *Antiques Journal*. May 1966, pp. 1-48.

Chevalier, M. Jean Guy, ed. *Antiques Journal*. June 1966, pp. 1-64.

Healy, Leslie L., "Hardships of the Early Pioneers of Richmond Township" (Que.), *Sherbrooke Daily Record*, March 14, 1953.

Hoekstra, Anne E., and W. Giles Ross. "The Craig and Gosford Roads." *Canadian Geographical Journal* 79 (2) (1969): 52-57.

Lombardi, Laura, Decorating ed. "Country Living on an Island (Ile d'Orleans, Que.)" *Country Living Magazine*, 126, 6 (April 1984): pp. 53-71.

Lombardi, Laura, Decorating ed. "Quebec Cottage." *Country Living Magazine*, October 1985, pp. 67-72.

Lombardi, Laura, Decorating ed. "Canadian Country Classic" *Country Living Magazine*, January 1986, pp. 60-66.

McLean, Eric. "Early French-Canadian Furniture." *The Magazine Antiques*, 1967, pp. 72-77.

Minhinnick, Jeanne. "Canadian Furniture in the English Taste, 1790-1840." *The Magazine Antiques*, 1967, pp. 85-90.

Minhinnick, Jeanne. "Country Furniture—A Symposium." *The Magazine Antiques*, 1968, pp. 351-354. (Country furniture in Upper Canada).

Richmond, Brian P. "Canadien Furniture." *Ontario Showcase*, August 1979, pp. 67-73.

Richmond County Historical Society. "The Trend of Pioneers." *Annals of Richmond County and Vicinity*. 1 (Quebec), 1966).

*Ibid*, 2, (1968)

Rodgers, G.A. "Pioneer Mill Sites in the Châteauquay Valley", *Québec Historie*, April, May, June, 1971, pp. 50-54.

Stein, Aron Marc, "French Influences in American Furniture." *The Antiquarian* 17 (1931): 15-19, 50, 60.

Thomson, MaryAnne, Field ed. "St. Genevieve: A French Village in Middle America." *Better Homes and Gardens Country Home*, August 1985, pp. 58-70.

Van Ravensway, Charles. "Missouri River German Settlements, Pt. 11, The Decorative Arts, 1831-1900." *The Magazine Antiques*, 1978, pp. 394-409.

Willis, James T. "Living with Antiques, Dundrennan Farm in Ontario." *The Magazine Antiques*, 1984, pp. 1434-1442.

Winchester, Alice. "French Canadian Furniture." *The Magazine Antiques*, 1944, pp. 238-241.

Winchester, Alice. "The Armoires of French Canada." *The Magazine Antiques*, 1944, pp. 302-305.

# Index

# Price Guide

The prices shown here merely serve as a guide. Actual market prices vary from one region to another and from one antique market to another.

Country auction and dealer prices close to or at the source often are much less than retail prices in the more pricey Boston to Washington corridor, or Texas, California, Toronto, etc. The selling price of an item, whether sold at auction or at retail, is strongly determined by the piece's availability, demand, structural condition, and its aesthetics, including patina, original paint, etc. Prices quoted here, with some exceptions, are for pieces still available and of average or better condition.

## Blanket and Other Storage Chests and Boxes

Post-and-frame type, early 19th century (figure 1): $150-$400

Quebec "V" Chest (coffer), pine, early 19th century (figure 2): $250-$700

Dome-Top Boxes, pine, 19th century (figure 11): $75-$250

Small document boxes, pine, 19th century (figure 14): $65-$225

## Armoires

Examples with 8, 10, or 12 raised panels, post-and-frame construction, paint stripped and showing good patina, pine, early 19th century (figure 22): $2000-$4000

The same with original paint in good condition: $3800-$7500

Examples with 4, 6, 8, or 10 sunken or inset panels, pine, 19th century, (figure 24): $1000-$2750

Examples with St. Andrews Cross cut into 6, 8, 10, or 12 raised panels, pine, early 19th century: $4000-$8000

Plain board *armoire* (jelly cupboard) with one door mounted on either butt or fische hinges, pine, early or mid 19th century, (figure 31): $400-$750

Plain board *armoire* (jelly cupboard) with two doors, four shelves, pine, 19th century (figure 33): $725-$1400

## One-Piece Stepback Cupboards

Plain boards, no panels, butted and nailed, open above counter, two plain doors below counter, pine, last half 19th century: $450-$750

Four raised-panel doors, two above counter and two below; heavy cornice, original paint, rat-tail hinges, good proportions and balance, pine, early 19th century: $3500-$6500

Four sunken or inset panels with two above and two below; medium cornice, original paint, butt hinges, pine, mid 19th century: $1000-$1650

Similar to above, white ash, last half 19th century (figure 38): $700-$1300

## Open Hutches or Dish Dressers

Upper half open with molded trim, three shelves, two drawers beneath counter and above two paneled doors, flush to floor, pine, mid 19th century (figure 41): $1250-$2000

## Two-Part Cupboards

Empire, ogee curves, top with two doors each paneled, counter with two drawers and two paneled doors below, mixed wood, mid 19th century (figure 47): $400-$700

Upper and lower cupboard, each with two raised-panel doors, strong cornice, original paint, rat-tail hinges, good proportions and balance, early 19th century: $2000-$4500

Same as above with sunken or inset panels, butt hinges, old paint, pine, mid 19th century (figure 44): $1200-$1800

## Low Buffets or Sideboards

Empire, three drawers over three sunken-panel doors, case and drawers dovetailed, butternut, mid 19th century (figure 55): $600-$900

Victorian, two molded drawers over two sunken-panel doors, molded frame, mixed hardwood, last third 19th century (figure 58): $300-$600

Three drawers over three sunken-panel doors, paneled ends, pine, early-mid 19th century: $850-$1500

Two sunken-panel doors, scrolled skirt, plank ends, pine, mid 19th century (figure 54): $750-$1100

## Corner Cupboards

Two-part cupboard with two glazed doors over two sunken- (inset) panel doors, heavy top molding, butternut, mid-19th century (figure 61): $1200-$1600

Upper half open with shaped shelves. One or two cutlery drawers above two raised panel doors in lower half. Bracket feet with shaped apron between brackets, original paint, pine, early 19th century: $2800-$4200

Two glazed doors over two raised-panel doors, bracket feet, original paint, pine, early 19th century: $2800-$3500

## Chests of Drawers—Commodes

Empire bonnet chests were popular and used extensively (probably replacing the ubiquitous coffer) during much of the mid and late 19th century. A variety of woods was used, but birch and ash predominated. Flame birch and figured maple of great beauty was used in some better examples.

Bonnet chest, seven or eight drawers refinished, flame birch, Empire turned legs, mid 19th century: $1200-$1500

Bonnet chest, seven drawer, painted, ogee trim, ash, late 19th century (figure 66): $350-$650

Three-drawer chest, plank ends scrolled at base, shaped apron, framed top, butternut, early mid 19th century: $600-$1000

## Washstands and Washstand Commodes

Washstand with gallery, cut out for bowl, shelf and drawer near base, Sheraton legs, pine, early 19th century: $150-$250

Same as above, butternut: $100-$200

Washstand as above with shaped or ornamented gallery and towel bars: $200-$400

Washstand commode with shaped gallery, one wide drawer beneath counter and two paneled doors underneath drawer, towel bars, shaped skirt, pine, mid 19th century: $250-$500

## Tables

Work table, one drawer, taper legs, three-board top, ash and butternut, mid 19th century (figure 74): $300-$500

Work table (tavern type), one narrow deep drawer, taper legs, two-board top, pine, early 19th century (figure 73): $600-$1200

Work table in original paint, "H" stretcher base, one drawer, gently tapered legs, pine with birch legs, early 19th century (figure 80): $700-$1350

Draw table, heavy frame and legs, pine top with heavy chamfered birch legs, mid 19th century (figure 83): $350-$700

Refectory tables, with three, four, or five drawers, three- or four- board tops, heavy taper legs, about 10 feet long, pine (figure 88): $2000-$2500

Same with sawbuck base, no drawers, pine: $2250-$3250

One-drawer stand, Sheraton turned legs, birch and maple, second quarter 19th century (figure 92): $150-$250

Taper-leg candle stand with one drawer, pine frame, birch legs, early 19th century (figure 91): $200-$275

## Chairs

*Habitant* chair, three-slat, refinished seat with snowshoe weave, birch and ash or maple, mid 19th century, matched set of four (figure 105 or 106): $600-$800

*Habitant* chair, two-slat with cutouts, woven seat, flame birch and ash, mid 19th century, matched set of four: $600-$1000

Shaped plank seat, three or four half spindles, refinished, maple and pine, second quarter 19th century, matched set of four (figure 112): $400-$650

*Habitant* rocking chair, three slat, good seat, birch and ash, mid 19th century: $75-$115

*Habitant* rocking arm chair, Eastern Townships type, painted, last half 19th century, as found (figure 130): $75-$150

*Habitant* rocking arm chair, refinished, mixed hardwood (figures 126, 127): $185-$300

*Habitant* arm chair, master's, with arms, woven seat, birch and ash, early 19th century (figure 136): $700-$1100

Thumb-back, four-spindle high chair, old red, New England type, second quarter 19th century (figure 123): $150-$225

*Habitant* high chairs, reseated, mixed birch, maple, and ash (figures 121, 122): $150-$275 each

Children's *habitant* rocking chairs, as found (figure 124): $50-$150 each

Hutch or chair table, Anglo-American type, pine top, hardwood frame (figure 137): $1600-$2100

## Stools and Benches

High stools with three or four legs, birch, maple, and ash, as found, 19th century (figure 141): $35-$85

Low benches (foot stools or crickets), commonly birch or pine: $30-$75

Kneelers, mortise-and-tenon construction, as found, pine, mid 19th century (figure 143): $35-$75

Bench, Ile d'Orleans type, "H" stretcher base, plank seat, heavy frame, pine, late 18th and early 19th century: $1200-$2000

## Beds

Folding bed (*banc lit*), neoclassical, spindle back in birch and maple, pine body, mid 19th century (figure 146): $1500-$2000

Child's bedstead, two rails all around, simple design, mortise-and-tenon construction, thick pins, pine, mid 19th century (figure 149): $175-$250

Empire rope bed, birch frame, pine headboard, blanket roll at foot, four turned posts, second quarter 19th century (figure 151): $300-$600

*Habitant* cradle, four extended turned maple posts, birch rockers and pine frame, 37" long, early 19th century (figure 152): $250-$400

## Desks

Student's slant-top, lift-lid, mortise-and-tenon construction, pine, hardwood square legs, mid 19th century (figure 154): $125-$195

Similar desk, heavy turned legs, all pine construction, old red paint, mid 19th century (figure 156): $200-$300

Table-top office desk, two drawers, inclined writing surface, twelve pigeon holes above, mid 19th century: $400-$500

Similar desk on frame, pigeon holes behind two hinged doors, one or two drawers behind slanted and hinged writing surface, taper legs, early or early-mid 19th century: $1200-$1800

## Flax and Wool Wheels, Yarn Winders, Swifts

### Wheels

Flax wheel, Quebec type, 30" (more or less) in diameter, turned spokes and legs, iron foot pedal, birch and maple, late 19th century (figure 157): $175-$225

Flax wheel, Anglo-American type, 20" (more or less) in diameter, turned spokes and legs, wooden pedal, birch, maple, oak, late 18th and 19th century (figure 158): $200-$235

Wool wheel, 40" (more or less) in diameter, turned legs, plain or turned spokes, mixed hardwood, 19th century: $185-$225

### Winders and Swifts

Hand-cranked reel mounted between two upright supports, each mounted into a shoe foot, pine, 19th century (figure 163): $60-$90

Anglo-American type clock and click reel, three or four supporting legs, cherry or maple, early 19th century: $65-$155

Swift, four arms, vertical chamfered support post mortised into shaped wood block base, original paint, pine and hardwood, first half 19th century (figure 164): $55-$125

## Churns and Dough Boxes

Churn or food mixer, large tub with lid, contained between two planks, each cut out below level of base of tub to form bootjack or similar legs. Large crank outside of tub operates interior paddle, pine, middle 19th century (figure 170): $200-$300

Dough box with sloping sides, plank ends cut out to form supporting boot jack legs below base of box. Cleated lid, exterior molding at base of box, old paint, pine, early 19th century (figure 165): $195-$300

Similar to above, plank ends cut out to form supporting Empire style legs below base of box, refinished, pine, mid 19th century (figure 166): $200-$325

Dough box of post-and-frame construction with sides and ends mortised into square posts, pinned, old red paint, pine with birch legs, early 19th century: $300-$500

## Woodenware

Bucket or pail bench with topping board, two shelves rabbeted to upright sides, pine, as found, mid 19th century (figure 171): $175-$250

Same, with backing boards scrolled at top and with scrolled apron below lower shelf at front, refinished, pine, 19th century: $350-$450

Wall box, salt (*boite a sel*) with hinged lid, shaped crest, ash, late 19th century (figure 174): $85-$135

Wall box, salt, open type, shaped back with hole for attachment, pine, mid 19th century (figure 174R): $85-$135

Long wall box, possibly for knives, deep bin, shaped sides, hole for attachment, pine, mid 19th century (figure 176): $175-$235

Long wall box, four compartments, possibly used for candles, shaped sides and back, hole for attachment, original pine patina, late 18th or early 19th century (figure 177): $550-$750

Kneading tray with fence, pine, late 19th century (figure 173): $30-$45

Wooden implements for above: $10-$25 each

Small candle box, lift-off lid, butted and nailed, original paint, pine, mid 19th century (figure 180): $75-$125

Candle box, sliding lid, hand dovetailed, original pine patina, 19th century: $155-$225

Plug tobacco cutter, hand wrought, shaped guillotine-like blade on arm attached to wooden cutting board, wooden handle, 19th century (figure 183): $75-$125

As above, with plain cutting bar, 19th century (figure 184): $25-$45

Clock shelf, 30" wide, excellent scallop margin, wooden support brackets, shallow fence, butternut, 19th century (figure 186): $125-$200

Wall shelf, Empire style bracket supporting shaped and molded shelf, maple, mid 19th century (figure 187): $90-$165

Sugar mold, two hearts carved in pine or butternut, late 19th century (figure 191): $100-$150

Same, single heart: $70-$110

Same, bird (cock): $125-$175

Same, large initial (figure 190): $65-$95

Four-part, Bible sugar mold with detailed chip carving, birch, last third 19th century (figure 193): $200-$325

Butter mold, round, handled plunger, beaver carved pat, late 19th century: $85-$125

Hatchet cover, chip carved, initialed, pine, late 19th century (figure 194): $45-$75

Mold, five-compartment maple sugar block type, ash, late 19th century (figure 189): $35-$60

Drying rack, folding screen type beaded and chamfered, birch, late 19th century (figure 198): $45-$65

Quilt rack, small, mortise and tenon construction, shoe feet, pine, early 19th century (figure 199): $95-$145

Mortar and pestle, ash, early 19th century (figure 195): $75-$125

Punched tin apple drying box, pine, late 19th century (figure 196): $65-$90

Towel rack, wall mounted, brackets and wooden roll, pine and maple, late 19th century (figure 201): $55-$85

Game board, checker trays, original fence, initialed, hanging loop, original paint, pine, 19th century (figure 202): $250-$350

Game board, carved, original fence, no trays, unpainted, butternut, late 19th century (figure 204): $125-$175

**Children's Furniture**

Quebec children's play furniture has been actively pursued by collectors for years, resulting in its present-day scarcity.

Doll's table, turned legs, molded top and apron, worn old paint, pine and birch, last third 19th century (figure 206): $85-$150

Child's toy *armoire*, four inset panels, solid ends, shaped apron, original paint, good proportions, pine, second quarter 19th century: $585-$900

Child's toy Empire bonnet chest, seven drawers, ogee trim, pine, late 19th century (figure 211): $185-$250

Child's doll cradle, four extended posts with knob ends, heavy rockers, board sides and ends, old paint, pine, early 19th century (figure 207): $185-$255

Pipe tongs, forged iron (figure 213): $20-$30

Serpent end pokers, forged iron knob or loop handles (figure 214): $20-$35

Wooden candlesticks, turned, white over old red paint, pine, early 19th century (figure 212): $55-$125 pair